Grace
– in –
His Bosom

HENRY A. FAGBOLA

ISBN 978-1-63961-852-1 (paperback)
ISBN 979-8-88943-753-6 (hardcover)
ISBN 978-1-63961-853-8 (digital)

Copyright © 2022 by Henry A. Fagbola

All rights reserved. No part of this publication may be reproduced, distributed, or transmitted in any form or by any means, including photocopying, recording, or other electronic or mechanical methods without the prior written permission of the publisher. For permission requests, solicit the publisher via the address below.

Christian Faith Publishing
832 Park Avenue
Meadville, PA 16335
www.christianfaithpublishing.com

Printed in the United States of America

Contents

Dedication v
Introduction vii

Relationship 1
Information 12
Knowledge 62
Communication 159
Distraction 173
Intimacy 192
Bonding 216

Dedication

This book is dedicated to the loving memories of my grand parents late Chief Thomas Akweke Oji and Oyidiya Susan Akweke Oji; who first pointed me to Jesus Christ.

Introduction

The nudging to get spiritual understanding resonated in my soul in the fall of 1998. On that fateful morning at the Living Faith Church Worldwide, Lagos, Bishop David Oyedepo taught extensively on Proverbs 4:7–9 and brought refreshing insights to the passage.

"Wisdom is the principal thing; therefore get wisdom: and with all thy getting get understanding. Exalt her, and she shall promote thee: she shall bring thee to honour, when thou dost embrace her. She shall give to thine head an ornament of grace: a crown of glory shall she deliver to thee." That passage produced more questions than answers.

I reckoned that if God in His infinite wisdom asked us to get something and, with that, get yet another, then such a venture must be worth all the efforts in the world. A thorough examination of the benefits associated with getting the twin jewels of wisdom and understanding led to my conclusion that, if that be all that I could get in my kingdom journey, so be it. From that moment, it was clear to me that there were activities associated with getting spiritual understanding.

After that profound encounter with the Word, I did not return to my former place of worship. I devoted myself to kingdom service at the Winners Chapel even as the search for materials that could lead me toward the path of spiritual understanding commenced. To my surprise, there are many publications on understanding anything but spiritual understanding. Put succinctly, there was a relative dearth of publication on the subject of spiritual understanding. Again, that discovery became the added impetus that led to my undertaking to publish the book in your hand. This text will bless you.

Relationship

Relationship is the greatest equitable wealth you can have. Relationships are sustainable. As you grow, so should your associations. Revenues come out of relationships. Money is in the relationship. Basically it is who you know and how they think about you. You can get anybody to attend your program if you have enough equity in character, integrity, honesty, and trust.

Everything God created and commanded to be fruitful, He did so based on relationship. Be fruitful, multiply and replenish the earth is a divine command predicated upon relationship (Gen. 1:28). In all the resources of production, people are the most important. People you relate to can either contribute to your growth or drain you.

God's creative power points to His redemptive love. God calls the world into existence. That must be viewed as an act of generosity. When God formed Adam in Genesis 1:27, He was in constant fellowship with Adam. Conscious that Adam should be in a relationship, The LORD said, "It is not good for the man to be alone. I will make a helper suitable for him" (Gen. 2:18).

Gleaning from that scripture, your relationship must be "a helper suitable for you." God is not only your helper but your help. "I will lift up my eyes unto the hills, from whence cometh my help, my help cometh from the Lord which made heaven and earth" (Ps. 121:1–2). Therefore, God has called you to a relationship by His redemptive power and love.

Call to Relationship

"My son, if thou will receive my words and hide my commandments with thee" (Prov. 2). That passage is an emphatic call to relationship. God intends that you should enter into a Father-son relationship with Him. God is a Father ready to do anything for an obedient son. Nonetheless, God left you with the power of choice. Consider the word *if* in the above scripture. God used that word because He wants you to enter into a relationship with Him out of a willing heart.

Variously in the Bible, God referred to man as little children, friends, and even gods. When God took the human flesh in Jesus, He called Himself "the Son of Man." The other son in the scripture is the one that we call the prodigal son. In that story in Luke 15, God also gave the prodigal son the power of choice, which he completely exercised.

He requested a portion of his inheritance and got it. He led a riotous life and descended the slope of failure on roller skates. However, when he returned from the dunghill of shame, the Father ran to meet him. That is the picture of God running to receive a son. The story of the prodigal son epitomizes God as the all-providing, all-loving, all-caring, and all-forgiving Father. God probably danced with His son on that day.

In the Bible, God is revealed in the power and beauty of creation. God is also revealed in the hearts of those who listen to Him. Having been made in the image and likeness of God, a call to relationship is indeed a call for you to reveal yourself to Him.

God is saying, if you desire the precious gift of understanding, you must, as a matter of priority, enter into a relationship with Him. He poured out Himself in a book called the Bible. He commanded you to read thoroughly and "hide my commandments in your heart." Truth is, the Bible is a book that you don't read per se. Instead, the Bible reads you. When you read the Bible, the Bible reads you inside out.

Why the call to relationship. First, the Trinity: Father, Son, and the Holy Spirit is all about a divine tripartite relationship. Second, without a relationship, it would be impossible for you to love God and your neighbors. Lastly, love defines the character of God and it is rated above faith and hope. God is love (1 John 4:8 and 16).

God desired a personal relationship with you. That desire defined the whole essence of creation. It is for that reason that He gave His only Son to die a gruesome death on the cross in order to rescue our souls from sin (John 3:16). The personal relationship God desires with you must come through His Son—the Lord Jesus Christ. He predestined us to be conformed to the image of His Son (Rom. 8:29). God does not intend to be a distant Father in heaven. His desire is to be a personal God living in the inside of you—His son.

Furthermore, God, through the blood of His Son Jesus Christ, abolished death on the cross of Calvary. But God didn't abolish sin. He paid for your sin via the blood of the Lamb that knew no sin. If you trust Jesus, you can face death. To be absent from the body is to be present with the Lord (2 Cor. 5:8).

The nature of man is heavily corrupted by sin and your sins have separated you from God. Jesus went to the cross and paid for all your sins. Additionally, He gave us the gift of righteousness as a covenant heritage. All you need to do is to stand on the righteousness of Christ and ask for forgiveness. No man can change his sinful nature.

The scripture says, "The soul that sinneth shall die" (Ezek. 18:20). But the moment you ask for forgiveness, you are forgiven. You are continually cleansed by the blood of Jesus Christ. You can do nothing to change your sinful nature but to continually ask for forgiveness based on what Jesus Christ did on Calvary. When you confess and accept Jesus as your Lord and Savior, your sins are forgiven. It's your covenant right which is automatic and precedent upon your confession. As soon as you do that, there's no more guilt.

Guilt is a step away from shame. God abhors shame. That's why He wants to pull that guilty past experience out of you. Sin in man is like the remote control in the hands of the devil. Guilt is like the sensor—that tiny object that binds the remote control with the thing it is supposed to control. If guilt is out of the heart of man, then there cannot be any form of control. When you confess, God will pull that sensor (guilty experience) out of you hence disconnecting you from the control of the devil. Jesus said the enemy came to me but found nothing. The prince of this world could not control Jesus because of the absence of sin.

If you choose to remain in the guilt of past experience, soon it graduates to shame. The good news is that Jesus calls you by your name and not by your shame. You are the righteousness of God in Christ Jesus. Quit struggling to live trusting those who you consider unavoidable because of the shame of failure. Trust Christ your Redeemer and the Rock of Offence.

> Wherefore also it is contained in the scripture, Behold, I lay in Sion a chief corner stone, elect, precious: and he that believeth on him shall not be confounded. Unto you therefore which believe he is precious: but unto them which be disobedient, the stone which the builders disallowed, the same is made the head of the corner, And a stone of stumbling, and a rock of offence, even to them which stumble at the word, being disobedient: whereunto also they were appointed. But ye are a chosen generation, a royal priesthood, an holy nation, a peculiar people; that ye should shew forth the praises of him who hath called you out of darkness into his marvellous light. (1 Peter 2:6–9)

God calls you "My son." That is indicative of the highest level of intimacy. In the scripture, things such as names, places, and time are open-ended. God allows that so that you can fill in your name, city, or year. Essentially, God says, "My son, Henry, attend to My Word."

There's nothing lower in ranking than shame. In Joel 2:26, God says, "My people shall not be ashamed." Jesus was despised and rejected by men. They asked even derisively; was that not the son of a carpenter? Can anything good come out of Nazareth? (John 1:46). We esteemed Him not. "He is despised and rejected of men; a man of sorrows, and acquainted with grief: and we hid as it were our faces from him; he was despised, and we esteemed him not" (Isa. 53:3). Whosoever believe in Him shall not perish but have everlasting life (John 3:16). A vital ingredient of everlasting life is one devoid of shame. Specifically, God addressed that crucial factor in Romans 10:11: "For the scripture saith, Whosoever believeth on him shall not be ashamed." Woah! What a promise.

In the valley of shame, Jesus took our infirmities and carried our sorrows and by His stripes you were healed (1 Peter 2:24). Jesus took the human flesh that He may demonstrate to us how to overturn and overcome the often negative judgment and condemnation of man. You too can do likewise by confessing Christ. Jesus completed the cleansing on the cross of Calvary. All you need to do is to receive it with your mouth wide open and He will fill it up (Ps. 81:11). "For I will give you a mouth and wisdom, which all your adversaries shall not be able to gainsay nor resist" (Luke 21:15). Use your mouth to confess Christ.

Relationship Road Map

Submitting to follow God is like joining the vehicle of understanding. The vehicle takes off from point instruction through knowledge to wisdom and understanding. Relationships thrive on faith. Obedience fuels the vehicle to destination grace. Grace is home to understanding. Put differently, understanding is wrapped up in grace.

However, before you arrive at the final destination, you'll no doubt go through the territory of the prince of the kingdom of Persia. It's at that point that your faith will be challenged. God loves relationships. The devil hates relationships. Satan thrives in disunity hence he will do everything to ensure that you either abort the journey or get distracted. You are not immune to it for our Lord Jesus Christ was tested. His victory came via the Word. Jesus's response to the distortion of the enemy was at every instance: "It is written." Truth is that you cannot resist the devil in the energy of the flesh. It is important that you learn and grasp that which "is written."

Word in Your Heart Is a Weapon

From the beginning, God asked you to hide His commandments in your heart because at the critical time, it's what you know against the distortions of the enemy. The intent of the devil is to move you away from the will of God. Daniel was challenged but his persistent prayer and fasting, relentlessly fueled the vehicle of faith. God heard him and intervened by sending a reinforcement of angels to contend with the enemy. Notwithstanding, Daniel suffered a delay of twenty-one days in receiving what God dispatched on the first day the request was made. It's not wrong to say that multiple blessings are stocked on the way simply because someone aborted the journey. The antics of the devil will not stop because you're a pious Christian.

In anticipation of such ugly scenario, God asks you to hide His words in your heart. God knows that you will need it at some point in that relationship.

Call Is Personal

In Genesis 1:26, God created you in His image and after His likeness. You have a mind, emotions, feelings about things, and so on. He gave you the power of choices so that you can make decisions. God gave you the makeup such that you and I under the right conditions might have life and have it more abundantly. Furthermore, God challenged you to "come let us reason together" (Isa. 1:18). He did that because He was aware of the strength of materials He deposited in you. They are the same materials in Him hence God is saying, Son, you have everything that I have. Therefore bring your strong points on any issue and let us compare notes.

When you reason together with Jehovah, two things happen. First, you break barriers and dismantle defenses that inhibit intimacy with the Lord. Second, you completely succumb under the influence of supernatural intellect and divine manifestation, designed to humble you. The invitation to "come let us reason together" is meant to be a sober lesson in humility. God's ways are not our ways and His thoughts are not our thoughts either. They are higher (Isa. 55:9).

God does not need you. He wants an intimate relationship with you because He loves you. It's impossible to have an intimate relationship with someone you don't really know. Many people believe in God but don't really know Him.

Conscious of that, God poured out Himself in the book called the Bible. He doesn't want you to engage in a fruitless search of trying to know Him through other sources. With a passionate appeal, God directed man to His autobiography—authored by Him, about Him, and most importantly in His word.

In Proverb 2:1, God says, My son, receive my autobiography, sturdy it and learn everything about me, for that is the basis of our relationship. Notice that before you were born, He knew you. He consecrated you. He predestined you to be conformed to the image of His Son (Rom. 8:29). All the above put together doesn't foreclose the truth that as the relationship progresses, God is interested in watching you pour out yourself to Him in any language you choose. Notwithstanding, here's a caveat: your "autobiography" in the form of prayers, petitions and supplications must be according to God's will. That's why He volunteered His will to you in the first instance.

Lord's Chosen

God in His infinite wisdom elected to call every believer into a special relationship with Himself. Ephesians 1:4 says, "He chose us in Him before the foundation of the world to be holy and blameless in His sight." Speaking to His disciples, Jesus amplified that scripture viz, "You did not choose Me, but I chose you. I appointed you that you should go out and produce fruit and that your fruit should remain, so that whatever you ask the Father in My name, He will give you" (John 15:16).

First is the call. As you obey, you automatically enter into a relationship with God. The call is real and personal. So is the relationship. Notice the manner David experienced it in Psalm 139:15–17: "I will praise thee; for I am fearfully and wonderfully made: marvelous are thy works; and that my soul knoweth right well. My substance was not hid from thee when I was made in secret, and curiously wrought in the lowest parts of the earth. How precious are thy thoughts unto me, O God! how great is the sum of them!"

In Jeremiah 1:5, God says, "Before I formed you in the womb I knew you; before you were born I sanctified you; I ordained you a prophet to the nations." Jesus chose individuals from a variety of life situations and merged them into followers. You can also follow Jesus because He has chosen you before time.

Why God became a man in Jesus. To catch a glimpse of why God became a man in Jesus, let us listen to the terrifying fear of the man Job after he was vitiated by the words of his friends. Hear him: "For he is not a man, as I am, that I should answer him, and we should come together in judgement. Neither is there any days man betwixt us, that might lay his hand upon us both. Let him take his rod away from me, and let not his fear terrify me" (Job 9:32–34). Job was terribly frustrated that he could neither see nor touch God. Moreso, there was no mediator between God and man. For Job that was the crux of the matter. Job was enveloped by terrible fear arising from frustration he felt about a God he could neither see nor touch.

In answer to that, God in heavenly places decided to become a man in Jesus so that you and I can have a personal relationship with Him. Jesus is not God diminished. He is God in the body and in flesh relates to man. Jesus is the mediator between God and man (1 Tim. 2:5). "For there is one God, and one mediator between God and men, the man Christ Jesus."

The fear of the Lord is the beginning of wisdom (Prov. 1:7). The fear referred to in the scripture above is a fear borne out of divine adoration. It's not a terrifying fear of hopelessness. When you see the glory and goodness of God, you fear the Lord out of a humble disposition. Wrong relationships get you in trouble. Right relationship protects you. The name of the Lord is a strong tower and the righteous run into it and are safe (Prov. 18:10).

Information

Aware of the fact that the body of Christ is familiar with the word *information*, I rushed through the Bible concordance to find out if God ever used that word. To my surprise, I couldn't find anywhere in the Bible where the word *information* was used. The closest I got was inform/informed used variously in Deuteronomy 17:10, Acts 21:20, Acts 21:21, Acts 24:1, and Acts 25:15. That discovery was revealing.

Preachers and teachers of the gospel have for long used that word to describe the Bible. Some describe the Bible as the information bank of God while others say that it is a collection of information about God and His kingdom, yet a third group defined information as the signature of God.

It's amazing that God never used the word *information*. God used the word i*nstruction* to describe a collection of His word. It's hard to understand why Bible scholars and teachers have continued to use the word *information* when God doesn't say so.

It's important to note that God is God the Creator. No one understands a product like the manufacturer. He alone knows the strength of materials that He invested in the product. Consequently, it is His prerogative to choose the appropriate vocabulary that best describes the product. God calls His word instruction.

Instruction is specific whereas *information* is very general. There is no idle word in the Bible. Information requires a material medium but God's word transcends a material medium.

Oftentimes, *logos* leaps out of the material medium to become *rhema* in your heart. Bible instruction is the signature of God. Instructions are recorded in manuals; hence the Bible is a manual of instruction.

A look at the definition of the word *information* will help us address related issues that have infected the vocabulary of the body of Christ. Information is described as the collection, storage, processing, and dissemination of news, data, pictures, facts and messages, opinions, and comments required in order to understand and react knowledgeably to personal as well as to be in a position to take appropriate decisions.

Below is a list of elements of information. These elements are considered vis-a-vis their positions in the Bible: (1) news, the Good News (Gospel); (2) data, not in the Bible but lots of instruction to Noah and Moses (Gen. 6:13–21); (3) pictures—cognitive, mental images (Num. 33:52); (4) facts, not in the Bible; (5) messages, The Gospel message; (6) opinions, not in the Bible; (7) comments, not in the Bible.

Take every word captive. God enjoins us to take every word captive (Prov. 2:1). The reason is simple. If we fail to grasp the intended meaning of every word, we run the prospect of missing the promise. It's all about receiving.

You don't receive the things of God in a vacuum. You must believe in what you receive. It's not possible to receive outside the threshold of your belief. On the other hand, the enemy hatched a master plan to twist every word of God. If the devil can corrupt the Word of God, then the very act of receiving is jeopardized and rendered ineffective. Every promise of God meant for you stands released hence it is important that you take every word captive. You must learn and perfect the act of receiving.

The Bible is a book of promises as well as a book of receiving. The book is littered with fervent calls from a loving Father to His children to receive His blessing. God's blessing is destinations—you. Corrupted words can inhibit your receiving. It's important that you carefully consider God's choice of words. It's imperative that you apply them as intended.

According to Hebrews 2:1, "Therefore we ought to give the more earnest heed to the things which we have heard, lest at any time we should let them slip." Listen carefully to the things you have heard and draw meaning from every word of God. It's impossible to draw meaning in a vacuum.

Meaning comes through conversation. It emanates from a question-and-answer session. Proverbs 15:33 says, "The fear of the LORD is the instruction of wisdom; and before honour is humility."

God's choice of word. Consider the aforementioned seven elements of information. Of that number, only three were used in the Bible per se—news, picture, and message. Fact, data, opinions, and comments were never used in the

Bible. That implies that the Bible doesn't meet the requirements to be classified as information.

Expressly, God called His word instruction. Further review of each of those seven elements will help our understanding.

What Is News?

It's difficult to precisely define *news*. In a nutshell, news is whatever a news organization or an editor decides to publish or broadcast. It's what is worthy of knowing as determined by an editor and his organization.

To qualify as news, the following ingredients must be present: (1) communicative effects; (2) proximity or nearness to those who are concerned; (3) must interest or concern them; (4) must be recent, fresh to be appreciated; (5) must be factual; (6) must not be mixed with a reporter's opinion; (7) must not be fabricated; (8) must be an account of an event; (9) must be reported no matter when it occurred.

To a large extent, news is selected based on its timeliness or recentness, impact, significance, proximity, human interest, and so on.

Truthfulness is the first law of news. God is synonymous with truth. He calls His word truth. Communicative effect is fulfilled as you respond to the Speaker (God), in worship, praise, prayer, meditation, offering and so on.

The events of the Bible are forever closer to those who believe. It's of paramount importance and interest to them as it concerns their daily life and existence. The Bible is an account of an event concerning a King, His Kingdom, and His children. It's not a fiction or makeup story.

The forty reporters (writers) reported only the truth and nothing but the truth as witnessed by the Holy Spirit. The events of the Bible occurred thousands of years ago yet each time you read the Bible, it continues to acquire currency (timeliness) and has remained fresh forever. By all accounts the Bible qualifies to be called the Good News.

The Good News Is Now

The Good News is neither a daily news nor a weekly news. The Good News is now news. The scripture says as soon as the eyes of Cleopas and his companion were opened, they headed to Jerusalem in the hour, to tell the apostles. That's why you can't run out of business publishing the Good News because it remains forever current, timely, and personal. It gathers frequency as it travels.

So many publications have come and gone but if you are engaged in the business of publishing the Good News, it will outlive you. The King of kings and the Lord of lords is alive. He is eternal. He doesn't perish.

The Good News is truth and truth doesn't perish. The Good News reveals your faith as faith doesn't procrastinate. Faith is now. Faith is the heavenly currency, yes the medium of exchange with which you obtain something from God. Without faith you can't receive the Holy Spirit.

In the last day, that great day of the feast, Jesus stood and cried saying, if any man

> thirst, let him come unto me and drink. He that believeth on me as the scripture hath said, out of his belly shall flow rivers of living water. But this spake he of the Spirit, which they that believe on him should receive: for the Holy Ghost was not yet given; because that Jesus was not yet glorified. (John 7:37–39)

Rivers of living water speak of the Holy Spirit, the divine Author of the Bible. Happily, "As cold waters to a thirsty soul, so is good news from a far country" (Prov. 25:25).

Data. Granted, the Bible contains lots of figures and data, God never called them *data*. God simply commanded Noah, Moses, and many others. What we call data, God calls instruction. It's easy to discern why God did so. Mankind can manipulate data. In some countries, manipulation of census data, for instance, is a major source of crisis. Most often, data is used to strengthen facts.

Picture. Picture or image as a word is in the Bible. In Numbers 32:52, the word *picture* was mentioned. As you read the Bible, you are filled with cognitive mental images. Those are rhema pictures.

Fact. Fact stands for reality, actuality, and certainty. As a word, *fact* could not find a place in the divine vocabulary. The opposite of fact is falsehood. The subjective influence of man has for centuries turned facts to falsehood. Faith doesn't deny fact. Faith acknowledges the truth. The righteous live by his faith.

Between fact and truth

Whereas fact was never used in the Bible, truth was used about 240 times. Examples are found in Luke 4:25, 9:27, 12:44, and so on. Fact is subsumed under truth and shades lower than truth. On the other hand, truth is the attribute of God wrapped in one word. Truth stands for exact, accurate, definite, precise, well-defined, just, right, correct, strict, literal, undisguised, unexaggerated, faithful, constant, unerring.

Facts enable us to draw comparisons and conclusions. Nonetheless, as a believer, don't draw conclusions on any issue based on facts. Check it out with the Word of God. Truth will always prevail. Fact holds you to your past leading to anxiety, depression, and despondency.

The scripture says, "Be careful for nothing but in everything by prayer and supplication with thanksgiving let your request be made known to God" (Phil. 4:6). If you spend hours on television listening to news, you are prone to anxiety. What they call breaking news is always bad tidings. They are capable of causing depression and breaking you down. But that should not be your story.

Your life is in the hands of God, serve Him faithfully. "Those that are planted in the house of God, they shall flourish" (Ps. 92:13). The altar you patronize will control you. Don't permit the altar of facts to control you. Facts have the tendency of moving you away from the Word of God. As evidence pops up in your mind at every turn, hold firmly to the Word of God in your heart.

Consequently, a knowledge of the truth is knowing God. Jesus put it this way, "And ye shall know the Truth and the Truth shall make ye free" (John 8:32) Truth is not only God's nature but the person of Jesus.

Fact is subjective. It can be manipulated, mixed with human feelings, comments, or opinions. The cardinal principle of journalism is "Facts are sacred, comments free." Truth is sacrosanct because it's of a higher strata. Truth is eternal and everyone that is of the truth hears the Word of God (John 18:37). Whenever fact is juxtaposed against the truth, that fact will disappear. For instance, it's a fact that someone has cancer. That's a clinically proven medical fact. But "by his stripes ye are healed." That is the divine truth. When the truth shows up, that fact (cancer) will disappear. Truth changes fact for good. Truth is the light that shines in darkness and darkness comprehended it not (John 1:5).

Fact is that you have a problem but the truth is that God (The Truth) is bigger than your problem. Fact is subject to variations, but the truth is the same yesterday, today and forever. Fact can't stand the truth just as sin and holiness cannot dwell together.

I studied cartography. It has to do with the intricacies of map making and design. There is a map room cliche that says, "To tell the truth, you have to tell a little lie." That always pops up when, for instance, Cartographers use the same size of dots to represent two towns that are not the same in size and population.

Constrained by scale factor, the cartographer's product—the map—is influenced by human shortcomings. Just like maps, facts carry an air of scientific authenticity that may or may not be deserving. Fact is open to the subjective influence of man.

Conscious of that, scientists and researchers always introduce what they call margin of error. Margin of error implies that a little lie has taken place.

Notwithstanding, a lie is simply a lie. Pronto. There's nothing like little lies and big lies. What qualifies anything as a lie is simply a deviation from the truth, the constant and exactness.

God abhors lies in whatever shade. That explains why fact is subtracted from the vocabulary of the Bible. No doubt, scientific data are necessary for man on earth. We are fascinated by facts.

Fact versus belief

Perhaps no other word has been used more often by church people than fact. It's hard to understand why Christians are in love with the word *fact* when it has no place in the Bible. Fact as a vocabulary should be left to lawyers, statisticians, journalists, demographers, and so on. Those groups of professionals can vary facts, adopt it in different shades, hues, patterns, and meanings to prosecute their projects. The rest of the world could engage facts whichever way they choose but the body of Christ must drop it completely from their vocabulary. Fact has done collateral damage to one thing that Jesus passionately pleaded with us to do—believe. Fact has diluted our belief.

Facts may interest you but continually lay hold of truth. God calls His word truth. We dwell in the domain of truth. The devil is interested in corrupting truth, thereby reducing its intensity and lowering its efficacy. The motive of the enemy is to make it impossible for you to receive what God released to you. You can't receive it until you believe it. Your belief changes the fact. The economy of the Kingdom is belief-driven. It's believe and receive instead of demand and supply.

How to deal with fact. To deal with fact, you must possess a faith attitude. Having a faith attitude revolves upon your belief. It's what you believe that will change the fact. Faith is excised in the direction of your belief. God has blessed us with all spiritual blessings in heavenly places in Christ (Eph. 1:3). Our duty is to claim our blessing every day. Whatever God promised, the same He will perform.

According to Romans 4:17–21,

> As it is written, I have made thee a father of many nations, before him whom he believed, even God, who quickeneth the dead, and calleth those things which be not as though they were. Who against hope believed in hope, that he might become the father of many nations, according to that which was spoken, So shall thy seed be. And being not weak in faith, he considered not his own body now dead, when he was about an hundred years old, neither yet the deadness of Sara's womb: He staggered not at the promise of God through unbelief; but was strong in faith, giving

glory to God; And being fully persuaded that, what he had promised, he was able also to perform.

The life of Abraham points to the attitude of faith. We must emulate Abraham in his attitude of faith if we must deal with facts and claim the promises of God concerning us. God made that promise to Abraham in Genesis 17:5. But Abraham "staggered not at the promise of God through unbelief; but was strong in faith, giving glory to God" (Rom. 4:20). Abram of Genesis 17:5 did not wait for the promise to be fulfilled before he took on the new name—Abraham. The next time God called him, He did so by the new name, Abraham (Gen. 17:9). I perceive that the person reading this is having a change of name right now. They will see you and call you blessed. They will call you favor in Jesus's name.

Abraham confessed not the promise to make it happen. He did so as an attitude. If you make a routine of no prayer, no breakfast, in no time it becomes your attitude. Whatever you make your routine becomes your attitude. If you make a routine of memorizing one verse of the scripture a day, soon you will become a living epistle.

God is a God of order. There's no confusion with God. Everything about God is about principles. His principles don't fall irrespective of race, geography or position. God is no respecter of persons.

Here's the key. "We having the same spirit of faith, according as it is written, I believed, and therefore have I spoken; we also believe, and therefore speak" (2 Cor. 4:13). If you believe, you must speak.

Faith believes and therefore speaks. You are not speaking to make it happen or to make what you are speaking come into existence. You are speaking to believe. That's how it works for God's way is not the same as that of man.

His ways are higher as indeed His thoughts. "For my thoughts are not your thoughts, neither are your ways my ways, saith the LORD. For as the heavens are higher than the earth, so are my ways higher than your ways, and my thoughts than your thoughts" (Isa. 55:8–9).

According to Romans 10:10, "For with the heart man believeth unto righteousness; and with the mouth confession is made unto salvation. "Surely the Lord hastens (watches) over His word to perform it" (Jer. 1:2). So shall it be in Jesus's name.

The intensity of fact diminishes with time. Truth gains intensity with time. It shines and shines until the perfect day. Truth never fades.

Death of fact. Here's the demise of fact: "While we look not at the things which are seen, but at the things which are not seen: for the things which are seen are temporal; but the things which are not seen are eternal" (2 Cor. 4:18).

Understanding the above scripture will stab your doubt and take unbelief out of the way. Those facts that you are carrying about, in the form of negative reports relating to your health, finances, marriage, career, studies, and so on, are but for a season. They are temporary reports.

Consequently, do not own them up, do not possess them. For instance, do not say "my headache, my cancer, my kidney problem, my negative bank account, my failure report sheet." No doubt, they are facts but they can only survive or be sustained for a season. They are temporal.

Scarcity of truth. Mankind is daily confronted by emerging global darkness enveloping the world. Consider the coronavirus pandemic which has caused more deaths than either of the world wars. There's so much fact about its spread, potency and variants but not on its origin. The world is yet to arrive at an agreement concerning the source of such a deadly biological weapon of mass destruction. What a perfidy.

Nonetheless, the Gospel is the power of God unto salvation. There's the scarcity of truth and God is saying, can I find a man to stand in the gap, that my people be not destroyed (Ezek. 22:30). Can you be counted among the faithful that will respond: "Here I am, use me."

In John 14:12, Jesus says, "Verily, verily, I say unto you, He that believeth on me, the works that I do shall he do also; and greater works than these shall he do; because I go unto my Father." Perhaps, we don't really believe in Christ since we ain't really doing greater works than He did. What is wrong?

The challenge

The challenge is traceable to your misunderstanding of the nature of *truth*. We have come to believe that truth is the same as fact. The dictionary listed fact as a synonym for truth.

In a 2009 article on *Facts Versus Truth*, Waitsel Smith wrote, "The reason why miracles happen could be directly traced to the difference between FACT and TRUTH and the reason they don't happen is our failure to discern that difference." I completely agree.

Nonetheless, here's the tragedy. When you're in court to be admitted to evidence or testimony, you are required to "say after me, I...do solemnly swear to tell the truth and nothing but the truth. So help me God." Herein lies the greatest tragedy for faith people like you and me because over time we begin to equate fact with truth.

The treachery about the court scenario is that at the end, all cases are decided based on available fact and not truth. Sadly, in a manner that Apostle Paul warned we began even unconsciously to assume that fact is synonymous with truth. And that has done great damage to the one thing that Jesus enjoins us to do consistently and continually—*believe*. When that happens, you're receiving is in jeopardy.

Every promise of God is at the mercy of your belief. Faith, which is exercised in the direction of your belief, does not deny fact but acknowledges truth. If you believe wrongly, your faith will be misplaced.

Consequently, you cannot receive what you asked for because half obedience is indeed disobedience. If you don't receive, it follows that you will lack evidence.

Without testimony, how can you model Christ? With what are you going to disciple the next generation? Missionaries without testimonies are often recalled from the mission field. The command has gone forth: "GO." The power to succeed is resident in those two letter words. Until you "GO," nothing happens.

Truth as the attribute of God. Truth as the attribute of God can be condensed into three broad categories: (a) attributes of relationship: God is faithful, God is constant, God is unerring. (b) Attributes of ability: God is exact, God is accurate, God is definite, God is precise, God is well-defined. (c) Attributes of integrity: God is just, God is right, God is correct, God is strict, God is literal.

Truth as a person. Truth never changes. "Jesus is the same yesterday, today and forever" (Heb. 13:8). During His kangaroo trial, Jesus barely spoke on three things: (a) His message (John 18:20–23), (b) His Kingdom, and (c) *truth.*

> Jesus answered, My kingdom is not of this world: if my kingdom were of this world, then would my servants fight, that I should not be delivered to the Jews: but now is my kingdom not from hence. Pilate therefore said unto him, Art thou a king then? Jesus answered, Thou sayest that I am a king. To this end was I born, and for this cause came I into the world, that I should bear witness unto the truth. Every one that is of the truth heareth my voice. (John 18:36–37)

Pilate was unaware that *truth* was standing before him because it takes faith to see truth. Whereas it takes nothing to believe, in fact, it takes faith to believe in truth. Truth is something which cannot be seen, yet it's real. Facts are basically things which can be seen. Proverbs 12:17 says, "He that speaketh truth sheweth forth righteousness: but a false witness deceit."

Christ is our Righteousness. We are righteous for Christ imputed righteousness to us. "But of him are ye in Christ Jesus, who of God is made unto us wisdom, and righteousness, and sanctification, and redemption" (1 Cor. 1:30). God who cannot lie is *truth*. "In hope of eternal life, which God, that cannot lie, promised before the world began" (Titus 1:2).

The knowledge of the truth gives freedom. It gives liberty. "And ye shall know the truth, and the truth shall make you free" (John 8:32). Love is located in the truth. "The elder unto the well-beloved Gaius, whom I love in the truth" (3 John 1:1).

God gave the world the Truth. Truth is the person of Jesus Christ. "For God so loved the world, that he gave his only begotten Son, that whosoever believeth in him should not perish, but have everlasting life" (John 3:16).

His word against another. He found no one higher to swear unto hence God swore by Himself.

> And said, By myself have I sworn, saith the LORD, for because thou hast done this thing, and hast not withheld thy son, thine only son: That in blessing I will bless thee, and in multiplying I will multiply thy seed as the stars of the heaven, and as the sand which is upon the sea shore; and thy seed shall possess the gate of his enemies; And in thy seed shall all the nations of the earth be blessed; because thou hast obeyed my voice. (Gen. 22:16–18)

God is the Almighty. The *I Am that I Am*. His opinion is His word. He doesn't measure His word against that of any other god or person. That's why the Bible makes reference to no other book. On the other hand, other books make reference to the Bible. As a man or woman, you are subject to opinion. Everyone holds an opinion about a subject or an issue. God is interested in what holds you and conviction.

Comment

is the synonym of *opinion*. Comment is your subject or issue. It's the reflection of your ue. God is not a commentator but the f. The Bible is a message of His command, instructions and promises to His children. The word *comment* is not in the Bible. God spoke expressly. His word is truth and needs no comment from Him. Psalm 119:89 says, "Forever, O LORD, thy word is settled in heaven."

Instruction

> My son, if thou wilt receive my words, and hide my commandments with thee; So that thou incline thine ear unto wisdom, and apply thine heart to understanding; Yea, if thou criest after knowledge, and liftest up thy voice for understanding; If thou seekest her as silver, and searchest for her as for hid treasures; Then shalt thou understand the fear of the LORD, and find the knowledge of God. For the LORD giveth wisdom: out of his mouth cometh knowledge and understanding. (Prov. 2:1–6)

The passage above is a divine call for you to read the Bible. The Bible is the book of God's words. It's the instruction bank of the kingdom community. In Proverbs 4:13, God enjoined you to take fast hold of instruction; let her not go: keep her for she is thy life. And in Proverbs 4:20, God says, "My son attend to my words; incline thine ear unto my sayings."

GRACE IN HIS BOSOM

Between instruction and information

Throughout the Bible, the Word of God is referred to as instruction. The Bible is the manual of life from a Creative Father to His children. Manuals are direct and specific whereas information is very general. There's no idle word in the Bible. With information you can edit, picking only those that are relevant to you or your situation. You can't edit the Word of God and expect to obtain the promises therein.

In Proverbs 4:1, God says, "Hear, ye children, the instruction of a father and attend to know understanding." God referred to His Word as instruction. Instructions are intended to direct and guide you toward achieving a set objective and goals. "Take fast hold of instruction; let her not go: keep her; for she is thy life" (Prov. 4:13). The promise of a glorious destiny in Christ is not without an instruction manual to direct your path.

The instruction God provided is universal. Under the right conditions—in this case, obedience—you can obtain the same result anywhere irrespective of geographical location, race, family background or language. God is no respecter of persons. He is not a man that He should lie neither the son of man that He should repent (Num. 23:19). He remains the same yesterday, today, and forever.

When you instruct someone, you give directions to, you order, you command, and/or train that individual. The Bible instruction is a road map to destination grace. On the other hand, when you inform someone, you communicate facts to, you make known to. Information may be intended to instruct. While information is discretionary, instruction is expedient. It is to be obeyed.

In an attempt to edit, manipulate, and restructure sentences and words, you may filter the core of the message. It's not possible to do that with the Bible without destroying both the context and intended meaning. The instruction of God is a jewel of inestimable value.

Against that backdrop, God says, "Receive my instruction, and not silver; and knowledge rather than choice gold. For wisdom is better than rubies; and all the things that may be desired are not to be compared to it" (Prov. 8:10–11).

God's word is accountable to Him only. God says in Isaiah 55:11, "So shall my word be that goeth forth out of my mouth: it shall not return unto me void, but it shall accomplish that which I please, and it shall prosper in the thing whereto I sent it." That implies that every word spoken by God is intended to produce results.

Put succinctly, every word will be judged by the result it produces. God's words will stand trial before Him. They are divine promises meant to minister to the hearts of His children.

In the Book of Acts 19:20; The word grew in that city and great was the harvest. "So mightily grew the Word of God and prevailed." In that context, the Word of God was described as a living organism hence it grew. A divine expectation is hovering over every word of God. God sows His word in the hearts of His sons. His word is divinely expected to grow and produce results.

Most importantly His word is expected to return to Him—the Speaker, with the expected harvest. Every word of God is on a mission and accountable to Him. Every word of God is in a hurry to fulfill its mission. All you need to do is to confess the word, and it starts to grow and will definitely deliver on purpose. God intended His word to produce results and fulfill its purpose in the life of faithfuls, and they never fail.

Evidence matters

Jesus went about doing good (Acts 10:38), but His disciples were not picking up the evidence or testimony. Perhaps they forgot to carry their cross. After all, He asked you to really "take up your cross and follow me" (Matt. 16:24).

The cross produces nothing but evidence. Conviction is birthed in the labor room or thrashing field of testimony. In the "abide in me and I in you," God is interested in what holds you to the vine. Conviction holds you. Conviction, evidence, and testimony are synonyms. They are the same and I have used them interchangeably in this context.

If you pick up your cross and follow Jesus, you will develop among others, the virtue of patience which is the direct outcome of perseverance and persistence in the midst of storms. The storms, the challenges will always pop up. That you are a good man, would not change that. Jesus might even be asleep as was the case in Matthew 8:23 when the storm arose. It was the duty of the frightened disciples to wake up the Master.

Similarly, it is your duty to keep Him awake through prayers and supplication. It is dangerous to assume that Jesus will not sleep while the storms of your life are raging. When the disciples woke Him up, He declared peace and there was calm. Again, Jesus says, "These things I have spoken unto you, that in me ye might have peace. In the world ye shall have tribulation: but be of good cheer; I have overcome the world" (John 16:33).

The storm test. When the other form of storm came, Jesus put a test to His disciples. Both Philip and Andrew failed because they had no evidence.

> When Jesus then lifted up his eyes, and saw a great company come unto him, he saith unto Philip, Whence shall we buy bread, that these may eat? And this he said to prove him: for he himself knew what he would do. Philip answered him, Two hundred pennyworth of bread is not sufficient for them, that every one of them may take a little. One of his disciples, Andrew, Simon Peter's brother, saith unto him, There is a lad here, which hath five barley loaves, and two small fishes: but what are they among so many? (John 6:5–9)

Listen, brethren. The disciples were with Jesus in John 2, where He turned water into wine and that was recorded as the first miracle. Even John 6:2 emphasizes that "a great multitude followed him, because they saw the miracles which he did on them that were diseased."

Jesus all along, harvested testimony but the disciples failed to take them captive. Jesus emphasized the need for them to bear witness with concrete evidence. "And ye also shall bear witness, because ye have been with me from the beginning" (John 15:27). Yet another Scripture say, "And they overcame by the blood of the Lamb, and the word of their testimony and loved not their lives unto death" (Rev. 12:11).

I reckon that they momentarily forgot all about that. Philip saw the multitude whereas Andrew empathized and in the process found a lad with five loaves and two small fishes. However, a big *but* followed his discovery. Result: their belief was tainted and faith diluted. While Andrew wore the faith of a questioning optimist, Philip, on the other hand had the faith of a pessimist. A questioning faith cannot produce evidence.

On the other hand, when Jesus lifted the seed and gave thanks, the atmosphere changed from not enough to overflowing. The positive faith of Jesus is the faith that makes things happen. It is the faith that declares "for with God all things are possible."

A Christian life without testimony is tantamount to wreckage. That must not be your story in the name of Jesus.

Of sealed and unsealed evidence

God will not require anything from you that you don't already have. Without controversy, God's purpose remains the rulership of the seen world from the unseen. Christ in you remains forever the hope of glory.

In Jeremiah 32, something extraordinary with immense spiritual significance took place. The accurate implication of that monumental event seems to have eluded the attention of the body of Christ for far too long. God chose to distinguish the evidence. He distinguished truth from fact. "And I subscribed the evidence, and sealed it, and took witnesses, and weighed him the money in the balances. So I took the evidence of the purchase, both that which was sealed according to the law and custom, and that which was open: And I gave the evidence of the purchase unto Baruch the son of Neriah, the son of Maaseiah, in the sight of Hanameel mine uncle's son, and in the presence of the witnesses that subscribed the book of the purchase, before all the Jews that sat in the court of the prison. And I charged Baruch before them, saying, Thus saith the LORD of hosts, the God of Israel; Take these evidences, this evidence of the purchase, both which is sealed, and this evidence which is open; and put them in an earthen vessel, that they may continue many days. For thus saith the LORD of hosts, the God of Israel; Houses and fields and vineyards shall be possessed again in this land" (Jer. 32:10–15).

Jeremiah sealed a set of the evidence and left the other open. God instructed him to put both the sealed and the open evidence in an earthen vessel. That has huge spiritual implications. At this point, I would implore you to pause and to think; what sort of vessel you are.

In 2 Corinthians 4:7, the scripture says, "But we have this treasure in earthen vessels, that the excellency of the

GRACE IN HIS BOSOM

power may be of God, and not of us." If you are convinced that you are an earthen vessel or vessel made of clay, you are at liberty to join me as we accompany The Weeping Prophet to the house of the Potter. Rejoice for the treasure of the kingdom is in you, the earthen vessel.

> The word which came to Jeremiah from the LORD, saying, Arise, and go down to the potter's house, and there I will cause thee to hear my words. Then I went down to the potter's house, and, behold, he wrought a work on the wheels. And the vessel that he made of clay was marred in the hand of the potter: so he made it again another vessel, as seemed good to the potter to make it. (Jer. 18:1–4)

The Potter at work was symbolically the picture of God.

The open evidence that is tantamount to fact is left open to the manipulation of man. Man is fascinated by fact. We can play with facts, manipulate, add to, subtract from, vary fact, introduce what we call margin of error and so on. Fact is open to the subjective influence of man. Truth is, all the witnesses who were present during the transaction in Jeremiah 32, could never render the same account of what they observed. That is the tragedy of fact.

The kingdom is within you. God who created all matter, choose to put both evidence—the open and the sealed;

fact and truth within you, that they may persist many days. That's why faith doesn't deny fact.

However, faith acknowledges truth. The sealing is the work of the Holy Spirit. Only the One who sealed it could open it. Pilate could not see The Truth standing before him in spite of the warning from his wife simply because he didn't believe hence he missed the kingdom.

Fact as in open evidence or eye witness sent Joseph to prison. After all, his garment was found with Potipher's wife (Gen. 39:12). Joseph's faith could not deny it and such persists many days until his faith acknowledges the truth by divine revelations of dreams. In the same manner, Daniel was thrown into the lion's den because of open evidence. God sent His Angel and shut the lions' mouths because "innocence" was found in him (Dan. 6). Ditto the three Hebrew boys: Shadrach, Meshack, and Abednego. In the midst of the fiery furnace, they held strongly to the truth and God delivered them (Dan. 3).

According to Wikipedia, Annie Dookhan is an American convicted felon who formerly worked as a chemist at Massachusetts Department of Public Health Drug of Abuse laboratory and admitted to falsifying evidence, affecting up to thirty-four thousand cases. Imagine an extremely high number of innocent people sent to languish in jail simply because of a single person's deliberate act of wickedness. That's the tragedy of fact. Fact was admitted as credible evidence. Eyewitness error remains the single greatest cause of wrongful conviction nationwide, the advent of DNA testing notwithstanding. In all societies and cultures across the globe, eyewitness evidence remains at the top most strata of testimony in the Justice systems. Thank God for DNA. Nonetheless, DNA is shades away from the truth because it is controlled by human elements.

Stop looking for the kingdom elsewhere. The day that you discover the Truth, you have discovered the kingdom. The kingdom is the divine consciousness that you carry around. That consciousness that will never permit you to steal, kill, and destroy. The Kingdom of God is the governing influence of God that pervades your atmosphere. It is that work of love in you which creates the fire and force that changes everything within and around you. It is a kingdom of feast and participation is always open to whosoever. Another name for it is *grace*.

No blessing appropriated to "seeing is believing." By professing truth and celebrating fact, Christianity has suffered untold damage in her belief. When truth is corrupted, belief is diluted. That's why things are not working as they ought to. The result is a scarcity of testimony.

The mission of the devil is to steal, kill, and destroy. Notice that there is a progression in the agenda of the enemy. Seeing is believing is an earthly maxim that puts fact over and above truth.

That maxim is a direct affront on 2 Corinthians 4:18 and must be completely dropped by the body of Christ. In 2 Corinthians 4:18, the Bible states that "While we look not at the things which are seen, but at the things which are not seen: for the things which are seen are temporal; but the things which are not seen are eternal."

The definition of faith in Hebrew 11:1 made it clear that it is not about what you see but the unseen. "Now faith is the substance of things hoped, the evidence of things not seen." Evidence, testimony, or conviction relates directly to the unseen.

Jesus said to Nathaniel, "Because I said unto thee, I saw thee under the fig tree, believest thou? thou shalt see greater things than these" (John 1:50–51). Also, Jesus said unto "Thomas, because thou hast seen me, thou hast believed: blessed are they that have not seen, and yet have believed" (John 20:29).

There is no blessings appropriated to seeing is believing. The blessings rest on those who believe in the eternal things not seen. The treasures of the kingdom are hidden from the naked eye but open to your spiritual eyes. "God is a Spirit: and they that worship him must worship him in spirit and in truth" (John 4:24).

If we must model Christ to the world, it is imperative that we get past the basics, which is simply that truth and facts are not the same. We must hold it to heart that truth supersede fact. We must begin to confess that God is Truth. The opposite of truth is lies. God despises lies.

He counted lies as second to proud in the list of abominations. "These six things doth the LORD hate: yea, seven are an abomination unto him: A proud look, a lying tongue, and hands that shed innocent blood, An heart that deviseth wicked imaginations, feet that be swift in running to mischief, A false witness that speaketh lies, and he that soweth discord among brethren" (Prov. 6:16–19).

Clarity of the Bible

Every version of the Bible is intended to bring clarity of meaning to its readers and enhance their understanding. In doing so, caution should be excised when expunging words from the Bible. While we substitute words, context and meaning must never be compromised. Consider the following translations of Hebrews 11:1:

A) Now faith is the substance of things hoped for, the evidence of things not seen. (KJV)

B) Now faith is the assurance of things hoped for, the conviction of things not seen. (New American Standard Bible)

C) To have faith is to be sure of the things we hope for, to be certain of the things we cannot see. (Good News Bible)

Notice that versions A and B have the same number of fifteen words whereas version C had twenty-two words.

The New American Standard Bible substituted only two words from that of King James Version. The two words are *substance for assurance* and *evidence for conviction*. No damage done to the structure of the sentence. The Good News Bible is written in what they call Today's English. It made use of simple and familiar words, which no doubt, makes reading pleasurable. Nonetheless, it added seven new words to that of KJV in the scripture under consideration.

In the process it sacrificed a particular word which by my estimation is central not only to the definition of faith but most importantly to its operations. That word is *now*.

Now as a word may appear loose and simple but God chose to put it at the beginning of that scripture in Hebrews 11:1. Now is everything to faith operation. Indeed God uses the foolish things to confound the wise. "But God hath chosen the foolish things of the world to confound the wise; and God hath chosen the weak things of the world to confound the things which are mighty" (1 Cor. 1:27).

I have the double set version of the Good News Bible. The bold prints and the easy-to-read style make it very attractive for me. Nonetheless, I don't understand why the translators of the Good News Bible chose to expunge the word *now* from that scripture. I am not a grammarian. My background is somewhat technical hence my grammar, mechanical. Nevertheless, the Bible is not just about grammar. It's about logos and rhema. The Word of God is light. It is truth as well as life.

Bible as a Book

The Bible as a book is the oldest medium of mass communication. The topic of the Bible is about a King, a Kingdom, and His royal offspring. The Bible is a unique book of history. It documents thousands of years of God's dealings with His subjects (sons). Bound in hardcover, paperback, or cloth, it took a longer time to produce (over two thousand years) than any other publication in history. Some regard the Bible as a book of ethics because it

GRACE IN HIS BOSOM

contains over six hundred judicial, domestic, moral, and religious laws and regulations that God gave the nation of Israel. Others consider the Bible to be a spiritual guidebook that reveals the mind of God. Interestingly, the Bible is all of the above descriptions rolled together.

Listen to what the Bible says of itself. "All scripture is given by inspiration of God, and is profitable for doctrine, for reproof, for correction, for instruction in righteousness: That the man of God may be perfect, thoroughly furnished unto all good works" (2 Tim. 3:16–17). Essentially, the Word of God and everything contained therein, whether it is historical, philosophical, legal, or spiritual counsel, is not only valuable but precious. The Bible is far more than a collection of helpful information. It is beyond a theology of place and people. The Bible is uniquely the signature of God. It is revelation from God to mankind that provides practical, divinely inspired counsel for daily living. Most importantly, it reveals God's purpose for creation and depicts how He will deal with the issues of poverty and other human challenges.

The theme, indeed the whole essence of the Bible is summed up in the first few sentences of the model prayer Jesus bequeathed to us in Matthew 6:9–10, "After this manner therefore pray ye: Our Father which art in heaven, Hallowed be thy name. Thy kingdom come. Thy will be done in earth, as it is in heaven."

Insightful appreciation of the first two verses of what we call the "Lord's Prayer" revealed that it is fundamental to the following: (1) God in the image of a Father; (2) in heavenly places; (3) relationship (communication, conversation, or prayer); (4) worship (hallow His name); (5) His Kingdom (superimposing His Kingdom on earth); (6) His will (superimposing His will on earth).

In essence, the "Lord's Prayer" is about a heavenly Father, craving earnestly for a relationship in worship so that He will release His Kingdom and bring His will to bear on every decision that you make on earth. The beneficiaries are the sons of God and that includes you. Read the rest of the model prayer and you will discover how God brought you into focus.

When at the advent of radio and television, the book industry was almost thrown into a quandary, the Bible could not be threatened. They were developments which the Bible predicted with stunning accuracy. The Bible stood the test of time and has continued to bring to fore significant portions of our developments. We are daily confronted with the truth of God's word. The Holy Book remains the most important part of our lives as we daily learn from it. We are entertained by it and we possess whatever we desire by upholding the Word of God.

Also, the Bible survived major reforms among people and nations even as it became the object of political suppression and the stimulus for champions of liberation. It has remained among our most cherished possessions and have helped to lay the foundations of free societies. The Bible as a good friend can be looked up again without tiring of its acquaintance.

As you read the Bible, the Bible reads you inside out. There's always something new each time you look up the Bible. Truth is, you don't read the Bible with your eyes but with your heart; hence, the *logos* constantly evolving into *rhema*. The Word of God is registered in the hearts of His sons.

Lastly, the Bible was written by believers to believers such as you. It is the knowledge of God in relation to the self. The Word of God is clasped in the heart as well as before the mind. It is the knowledge of God as Redeemer as well as Creator.

Read the Bible

Isaiah 34:16 says, "Seek ye out of the book of the LORD, and read: no one of these shall fail, none shall want her mate: for my mouth it hath commanded, and his spirit it hath gathered them." Expectedly, people are worried about how to go about fulfilling the Lord's command as recorded in Matthew 6:33. "Seek ye out of the book of the Lord and read" is the breakthrough to "seek ye first the Kingdom of heaven and its righteousness and all these things shall be added unto you."

"How to seek?" must have been a common refrain of the people of Matthew 6:33. Today, Christians all over the world are confronted with the same question.

In "seek ye out of the book and read." God directed you to seek His Kingdom. He directed you to The Book. The Bible is the greatest book ever written in human history. God didn't only direct you where to find ways of His Kingdom, He requested you to read.

Seeking is never done without some sort of activity. Seeking of any sort is activity based hence God directed you to explore and exploit the Bible and mine the treasures therein.

As a book the Bible has no power. You must go beyond the book. It's never enough for the Bible to rest under your pillow, your car, office table either as a protective item, a symbol of identification or decorative item. The power is the word and not the pages. It's important to open the book and confront the Word.

God referred to everything in the Bible as "My Word" (Prov. 2:1). God loves the word so much that He called Himself the Word. God is so obsessed with His word such that He runs the whole universe with His mouth. He enjoined you to read the book because His word belongs in your heart. Your heart is the bank for the Word of God. His directive was for you to "hide my commandments with thee" (Prov. 2:1).

Furthermore, in Deuteronomy 6:6–9, God says,

> And these words, which I command thee this day, shall be in thine heart: And thou shalt teach them diligently unto thy children, and shalt talk of them when thou sittest in thine house, and when thou walkest by the way, and when thou liest down, and when thou risest up. And thou shalt bind them for a sign upon thine hand, and they shall be as frontlets between thine eyes. And thou shalt write them upon the posts of thy house, and on thy gates.

For the sake of His Word, God made a covenant. He did so that His words will be upon your heart and to write them in your mind.

Hear Him: "This is the covenant that I will make with them after those days, saith the Lord, I will put my laws into their hearts, and in their minds will I write them" (Heb. 10:16). He is a covenant keeping God.

As the beneficiary of that covenant, you have a part in the fulfillment. Your covenant right which rests in Christ, permits you to "seek out of the book and read." As soon as you open the Bible and apply your heart to the Word of God, that covenant becomes operational in your life. So shall it be in Jesus's name.

The people of Acts 17:11 understood the importance of the word. According to the scripture, "These were more noble than those in Thessalonica, in that they received the word with all readiness of mind, and searched the scriptures daily, whether those things were so." The New American Bible puts it this way, "Now these were more noble than those in Thessalonica, for they received the word with great eagerness, examining the scriptures daily to see whether those things were so."

They were described as noble because they willingly and eagerly received the word. They didn't stop at that. They continually searched the scriptures daily. That way, what was their routine became their habit. God wants you to live in that manner. Search the word until it becomes your habit.

The NASB started Acts 17:11 with *now*. The word *now* introduced a whole gamut of activity that is predicated upon your covenant heritage in Christ. As they discharged those activity-based covenant responsibilities, the next scripture was a testimony of their harvest. "Therefore many of them believed, along with prominent Greek women and men." What a harvest!

If in your relationship with God, you reached the point as the people of Acts 17:11, where you read, searched out, or examined the scriptures passionately "to see if these things were so," you are indeed at liberty to drop this book right now.

Congratulations for you are at the point of intimacy with God. The quest for intimacy borne out of zealous conversation with God is the threshold for understanding. Searching, examining the scriptures, meditating, and/or questioning is the seed for understanding.

God for a long time invited you to come let us reason together (Isa. 1:18). There's no other way to reason with God than to meditate on His word and approach Him with questions in some sort of bedroom conversation. He promised to answer when you call (Jer. 33:3).

Meaning is borne out of a question-and-answer session. That, in a nutshell, is how you arrive at the place of understanding. Therefore call *now*!

God transforms His Word

God spoke His Word to His sons and that includes you. He never intended that His word will remain dormant in a book. The Word of God was intended to undergo a transformation process. The three phases of word transformation are (a) written word, (b) spoken word, (c) living word.

(a) *Written Word*. On three occasions in Matthew 4:4, 7, and 10, Jesus used the written word as a potent weapon against the tempter—Satan. "But he answered and said, It is written, Man shall not live by bread alone, but by every word that proceedeth out of the mouth of God" (Matt. 4:4). "Jesus said unto him, It is written again, Thou shalt not tempt the Lord thy God" (Matt. 4:7). "Then saith Jesus unto him, Get thee hence, Satan: for it is written, Thou shalt worship the Lord thy God, and him only shalt thou serve" (Matt. 4:10). Notice that Jesus didn't defeat the enemy in the energy of the flesh. In all three occasions, He referred to the written Word of God.

Interestingly, Jesus didn't ask the enemy to tarry a little so that He could open the book. What was written was already in His heart. Of course they were His word. God put on the human flesh in Christ just to demonstrate in a simple but practical manner, how God wants you to deal with the enemy.

In plain language, God wants you to photocopy or better still autopage His word in your heart. The enemy is scheduled to come like a flood and at a time of your vulnerability. Definitely, there will be no time for you to consult the Bible or to even place a call across to your anointed pastor. Your victory is in what is written as embedded in your heart. The important question: what is it that you know?

Recall that before the fall, satan was some sort of a professor of Bible studies. He knows every word of God. Afterall, he was an archangel. At The fall, he chooses to corrupt the Word of God. The same tactics that he used on Eve at the Garden of Eden. Essentially, the battle against the enemy is one that is rooted in a thought process and those thoughts come as a string of emotions which aptly depicts what is widely known as temptations.

The battle is in your mind. The thought process is the conveyor belt between the mind and the heart. As soon as the word reaches your heart, it is settled. The heart of man is a guarantor of the measure of protection to the word. That's why God has ceaselessly pleaded with you to "hide My word in your heart."

Temptation is simply fulfilling a real need in a wrong way. Having fasted for forty days and nights, Jesus was vulnerable to hunger and taste. He was weak, dehydrated, and hungry. Jesus at that point had real needs. He would not succumb to that satanic influence by fulfilling those needs the wrong way.

Jesus reached out to the written word and the enemy departed after the third attempt. Thereafter, angels ministered to Him. If you must resist the devil, you must receive the word, hide it in your heart, and be ready to release your heavenly weapons in time of trouble.

(b) *Spoken Word*. In Isaiah 55:10 and 11, God spoke expressly about the power resonate in His word. Listen to Him.

> For as the rain cometh down, and the snow from heaven, and returneth not thither, but watereth the earth, and maketh it bring forth and bud, that it may give seed

GRACE IN HIS BOSOM

> to the sower, and bread to the eater: So shall my word be that goeth forth out of my mouth: it shall not return unto me void, but it shall accomplish that which I please, and it shall prosper in the thing whereto I sent it. (Isa. 55:10–11)

Creation began with the spoken word in Genesis 1. God created everything via His spoken word. Repeatedly God SAID before He SAW whatever He commanded.

God as a loving Father poured out His word to you. Your duty is to hide the Word of God in your heart and confess it via your mouth. "For with the heart man believeth unto righteousness; and with the mouth confession is made unto salvation" (Rom. 10:10).

Truth is, the Word of God was never spoken to be consigned to the sensory organ of hearing. Your ear is not a bank for the Word of God. The heart is where the word resides.

If the word must grow on earth, the ear-heart-mouth tripartite relationship must be fully functional and completely utilized. Granted that the word enters through the ear but it acquires its protective shield in your heart. "So then faith cometh by hearing, and hearing by the Word of God" (Rom. 10:17).

However, for the word to be settled on earth, you have to speak it out. You must vocalize the word because the Word of God is spoken to be spoken.

The scripture says that the Word of God is forever settled in heaven (Ps. 119:89). In enunciating the model prayer of Matthew 6:9, Jesus emphasized that point: "Thou will be done on earth as it is in Heaven." God's will is in His word, it's His word. God's agenda in that respect is simply that you should talk to Him. He wants you to do so on the basis of His word.

That's why He poured out His word in the first instance, in a book called the Bible. He pleaded with you to not only receive His word but to "take with you word" in all your dealings. To borrow a military parlance, the heart is the camouflage for God's word. As soon as your heart is saturated with the word, the only viable option is a release. Whenever the military uncovers any arsenal, that weapon is indeed ready for some sort of action. It must be put to use.

Happily, God gave you a mouth and a wisdom to which no adversary can gainsay nor resist (Luke 21:25). He directed you to "open thy mouth wide, and I will fill it" (Ps. 81:10). As a good soldier, your duty is to obey. Just open your mouth wide for the filling is done by the Holy Spirit, the Author of the word.

The Holy Spirit which indwells in you holds the trigger. He pulls the trigger from the deep recesses of your heart. That way, you will discover a whole new vista. It's impossible to exercise the dominion given to you in Genesis 1:26, 28 without speaking the word.

Be fruitful, multiply, and inherit the earth is a promise and all of God's promises relating to your life are hovering over you. They are at the mercy of your spoken words. They can't deliver on their own without being fertilized by your spoken words.

Jesus knew the word, He didn't stop at that. He spoke the word and satan departed from Him. In like manner, the Apostles spoke the word and the word grew. "So mightily grew the Word of God and prevailed" (Acts 19:20).

The word didn't only grow, it prevailed. So shall it be for you in Jesus's name. The word you know is not enough. For you to bring heaven on earth, you must speak the word. It's the spoken word that grows and God will always confirm the spoken word with signs following. "And they went forth, and preached every where, the Lord working with them, and confirming the word with signs following. Amen" (Mark 16:20).

In 2 Corinthians 4:13, the scripture stated that, "We having the same spirit of faith, according as it is written, I believed, and therefore have I spoken; we also believe, and therefore speak." If you believe, it's imperative that you speak. Speak according to what is written, speak according to what you believe. The beauty of the believer is in an open mouth which continues to pay the sacrifices of the lips.

Today, God will anoint your tongue with a coal of holy fire. As you say it, so shall you see it, in Jesus's name.

(c) *Living Word.* John 1:1–5 is about the Deity of Jesus Christ. "In the beginning was the Word, and the Word was with God, and the Word was God. The same was in the beginning with God. All things were made by him; and without him was not anything made that was made. In him was life; and the life was the light of men. And the light shineth in darkness; and the darkness comprehended it not."

The *Living Word* is Jesus Christ. He is the Word of life. "Sanctify them in the truth, Your word is truth" (John 17:17). And in John 14:6, "Jesus saith unto him, I am the way, the truth, and the life: no man cometh unto the Father, but by me." Again, "Jesus said unto them, Verily, verily, I say unto you, Before Abraham was, I am" (John 8:58).

Everything about your life as a believer, points to Jesus-The Living Word. Therefore look unto Jesus the author and finisher of our faith (Heb. 12:2). As Jesus steps into your life, every dark area of your life will disappear. So shall it be in Jesus's name.

The Bible is a book that you don't really read. The Bible reads you. All you need to know to have eternal life is Jesus. Cling tightly to Jesus for He is the Word of life.

It's important to give voice to the Word of God because the angels only hearken to the voice of the word (Ps. 103:20). In the word is the audible voice of God. He spoke in time past and He is still speaking today. You must pay attention to the connection between the voice, hearing, speaking, and listening. We understand that "So then faith cometh by hearing and hearing by the Word of God" (Rom. 10:17).

In Luke 9:35–36, "And there came a voice out of the cloud, saying, This is my beloved Son: hear him. And when the voice was past, Jesus was found alone...." The problem has never been with the voice. The challenge is whether you are willing and sanctified to receive the voice. You must be sanctified in the truth because His word is truth (John 17:17). Glory to God, there's no error in scripture. Some people may know the scriptures and still twist them. Nevertheless, the truth will always prevail.

The power of Jesus was not in what He said, but what was in what He said. In Luke 10:19, "Behold, I give unto you power to tread on serpents and scorpions, and over all the power of the enemy: and nothing shall by any means hurt you." If Jesus must die, He had to shut His mouth. There was so much power in what He says such that He decided not to talk anymore. Jesus was so much in a hurry to die for the sake of you and me even as He spoke no more. That He did that the scripture would be fulfilled. "He was oppressed, and he was afflicted, yet he opened not his mouth: he is brought as a lamb to the slaughter, and as a sheep before her shearers is dumb, so he openeth not his mouth" (Isa. 53:7).

John 19:10 puts it this way: "Then saith Pilate unto him, Speakest thou not unto me? knowest thou not that I have power to crucify thee, and have power to release thee?" Obviously Pilate was frustrated.

Nonetheless, the issue of power was so much dear to the heart of Jesus, such that He could no longer ignore Pilate. He had to let Pilate understand the source of power. "Jesus answered, Thou couldest have no power at all against me, except it were given thee from above: therefore he that delivered me unto thee hath the greater sin" (John 19:11).

Throughout that kangaroo trial, Jesus barely spoke on four issues: (a) His accomplishment in ministry, which was an open secret; (b) His Kingdom; (c) the truth; (d) power. All the above are core facets of Kingdom experience. First, you must be accountable to your call and calling. Your conduct and work should speak for you. Second, you must belong to the Kingdom and understand its functioning.

Third, you must know the truth and the truth you know will set you free. Lastly, you must be conscious of the power which God bequeathed to you in Luke 10:19 and exercise it, to the glory of God. However, power is transient. If per adventure you fail to utilize the power and fulfill its purpose, you are completely at the mercy of losing it.

Logos and *rhema*. *Logos* is the written Word of God. God wants you to read His word, hear His word before touching and feeling Him. *Rhema* is revelation. It's personal. *Rhema* is when logos come alive and relates to you; your experiences and circumstances in a personal manner. God doesn't want you to know Him personally without knowing what He says about you and your place in the Kingdom.

Repeatedly God says, "My son receive my word, hide them in your heart" (Prov. 2:1). The heart offers protection to the word as opposed to the mind. Jesus says the kingdom of God is like a grain of mustard seed planted in a field. In Luke 17:21 Jesus says, "Neither shall they say, Lo here! or, lo there! for, behold, the kingdom of God is within you."

The field or garden is within you. "Another parable put he forth unto them, saying, The kingdom of heaven is like to a grain of mustard seed, which a man took, and sowed in his field" (Matt. 13:31). A garden is to be tendered and protected. Most gardens have gates. In that manner, you can control what goes in and out.

Speaking to the generation of them that seek Him in Psalm 24:7–10, the Lord said,

> Lift up your heads, O ye gates; and be ye
> lift up, ye everlasting doors; and the King

> of glory shall come in. Who is this King of glory? The LORD strong and mighty, the LORD mighty in battle. Lift up your heads, O ye gates; even lift them up, ye everlasting doors; and the King of glory shall come in. Who is this King of glory? The LORD of hosts, he is the King of glory. Selah.

It is not a mistake that God repeated the same word. God has no error, no mistake and doesn't stutter. God is always in a hurry to bless you whenever your act of obedience pleases Him. He demonstrated that when He blessed Abraham. On that occasion, God's word was almost scrambling for position. He found no higher authority to swore unto hence He swore by Himself.

Thereafter, I perceive that the words scrambled for attention as they came cascading one after another, as in blessing I will bless you; and in multiplying, I will multiply thy seed.

> And the angel of the LORD called unto Abraham out of heaven the second time, And said, By myself have I sworn, saith the LORD, for because thou hast done this thing, and hast not withheld thy son, thine only son: That in blessing I will bless thee, and in multiplying I will multiply thy seed as the stars of the heaven, and as the sand which is upon the sea shore; and

> thy seed shall possess the gate of his ene-
> mies; And in thy seed shall all the nations
> of the earth be blessed; because thou hast
> obeyed my voice. (Gen. 22:15–18)

That to me was God stuttering. He was in a hurry to bless Abraham. Now, God is in a hurry to bless you. So shall it be in Jesus's name.

In Psalm 24:7–10, God is referring to the gates of your heart. That's where the garden is. That's where His word is protected, tendered and nourished. God is speaking to the gates and doors of your heart. He directs them to be lifted so that the Holy Spirit will take residence, in power and glory.

The things of God are hidden in the heart. Understanding is of the heart. Understanding is strategic whereas wisdom is tactical. Wisdom is for every day, every moment application. That explains why wisdom is referred to as the principal thing. "Wisdom is the principal thing; therefore get wisdom: and with all thy getting get understanding" (Prov. 4:7). God intends that after you have gotten the principal thing, you should get the strategic thing which is understanding.

The necessary desideratum of every power holder is to become an overcomer. Only overcomers possess their possessions. Already, the power is resident in you because you are standing on the righteousness of Christ. Power is released on the altar of holiness. You don't have to shut up your mouth.

Don't be a closed-mouth believer for Christ had done that for you before Pilate that He may salvage you from the debilitating scourge of sin without relinquishing authority to the enemy as the first Adam did in the garden.

God gave you a mouth and wisdom. Therefore, use it. Life and death are in the power of your tongue. "A man's belly shall be satisfied with the fruit of his mouth; and with the increase of his lips shall he be filled. Death and life are in the power of the tongue: and they that love it shall eat the fruit thereof" (Prov. 18:20).

Using your mouth to confess the word is, to God, a covenant. Listen to Him. "As for me, this is my covenant with them, saith the LORD; My spirit that is upon thee, and my words which I have put in thy mouth, shall not depart out of thy mouth, nor out of the mouth of thy seed, nor out of the mouth of thy seed's seed, saith the LORD, from henceforth and for ever" (Isa. 59:21). Both the bullet and the trigger are at your disposal. They are at the mercy of your willingness to deploy. Notice that the word and the Holy Spirit always agree.

Don't wait for miracles to happen. Strive to create the atmosphere for living in the miraculous. Through daily prayer soak yourself in the power and grace moment by moment. When you cling to the truth of His word, you will find power, strength and blessing even in the midst of infirmities. "Have not I commanded thee? Be strong and of a good courage; be not afraid, neither be thou dismayed: for the LORD thy God is with thee whithersoever thou goest" (Josh. 1:9).

According to Romans 8:11, "But if the Spirit of him that raised up Jesus from the dead dwell in you, he that raised up Christ from the dead shall also quicken your mortal bodies by his Spirit that dwelleth in you." Expressly, "Jesus answered and said unto him, If a man love me, he will keep my words: and my Father will love him, and we will come unto him, and make our abode with him" (John 14:23). As an individual, whatever you manifest is a function of He that is in you. If he that is in you is not greater than he that in the world, then you need to return immediately. Return to the base. Until you return, you can't see. "I returned, and saw under the sun, that the race is not to the swift, nor the battle to the strong, neither yet bread to the wise, nor yet riches to men of understanding, nor yet favour to men of skill; but time and chance happeneth to them all" (Eccl. 9:11).

On the other hand, if greater is He that is in you is indeed greater than he that is in the world, you got no option under the sun than to continually manifest His glory (1 John 4:4). You are not of your own. Something greater is dwelling in your inside which has a legitimate claim to your ownership. He holds the ownership title of you. That claim was amplified.

> What? know ye not that he which is joined to an harlot is one body? for two, saith he, shall be one flesh. But he that is joined unto the Lord is one spirit. Flee fornication. Every sin that a man doeth is without the body; but he that committeth

fornication sinneth against his own body. What? know ye not that your body is the temple of the Holy Ghost which is in you, which ye have of God, and ye are not your own? For ye are bought with a price: therefore glorify God in your body, and in your spirit, which are God's. (1 Cor. 6:16–20)

When a Christian receives the Holy Spirit, he has received power to cause changes. It's important that you meditate on the Word of God. In doing so, the word through the Spirit acts on your mentality. If meditation becomes your way of life, you will be the reflection of the Word of God. The "he that is in you" will show up at every turn of events.

Knowledge

"Yea, if thou criest after knowledge, and liftest up thy voice for understanding" (Prov. 2:3). The word *criest* in that scripture implies some sort of anguish. It's an *anguish of heart*. A burden to be lifted. It's the burden of ignorance.

Knowledge brings light and the light shines in darkness and darkness comprehended it not (John 1:5). Knowledge is the awareness of information. It's what you know.

At this stage of your Kingdom journey, God says, you must know me and my kingdom community. The knowledge of God comes from His word as recorded in the Bible. As you read the Bible, you gain acquaintance with God and recognize Him as the Almighty. That comprehension brings about familiarity.

As God sharpens your perceptive abilities, every instruction received crystallizes into knowledge. It's at the stage of knowledge that wisdom is wrought.

Wisdom is knowledge plus application. That confirms the short range, every day, every decision, every action usage nature of wisdom.

Nonetheless, there can never be knowledge without challenges. Those challenges are the burden hence the crying after knowledge. In practical terms, the anguish-of-heart is located in your study. No study, no knowledge. Study is the seed of knowledge (Prov. 18:15, 2 Tim. 2:15). Daniel understood by books (Dan. 9:2). The stage of acquiring knowledge of the kingdom is the most crucial in the life of the believer because it's the stage where you begin your journey of intimacy with God. The devil doesn't want that because he doesn't want you to join the army of great salvation. Knowledge is the awareness of facts, truth, or principles. It's what you know.

There are various ways of knowing something. They include but, not limited to cognition, acquaintance, familiarity, comprehension, recognition, perception, enlightenment, insight, consciousness, study, and apprenticeship.

Daniel studied books. Elijah mentored Elisha. The disciples understood through acquaintance and apprenticeship. Paul studied for he was Pharisee educated before he was apprehended by grace. Also, Paul mentored both Silas and Timothy.

God of knowledge

In 1 Samuel 2:3, the scripture says, "Talk no more so exceeding proudly; let not arrogancy come out of your mouth; for the LORD is a God of knowledge, and by him actions are weighed." God is a God of knowledge and His intention is that we should get to know Him via His word.

It is instructive to understand that "The heart of the prudent getteth knowledge; and the ear of the wise seeketh knowledge" (Prov. 18:15). Only fools hate knowledge and God doesn't respond to the cry of anyone who hates. "How long, ye simple ones, will ye love simplicity? and the scorners delight in their scorning, and fools hate knowledge? Then shall they call upon me, but I will not answer; they shall seek me early, but they shall not find me. For that they hated knowledge, and did not choose the fear of the LORD" (Prov. 1:22, 28, 29). God enjoined you to "turn you at my reproof: behold, I will pour my spirit unto you, I will make known my word unto you" (Prov. 1:23). God's words are in the book you have.

Open the Bible and read. Study His words and obtain knowledge of the King and His Kingdom. It's on the wings of such knowledge that His Spirit is poured unto you. God doesn't use the experience per se. He intended that you experience Him through His word. After which He will pour His Spirit unto you and qualify you. God doesn't need the qualified. He qualifies you with a call. "For His gifts and calling are without repentance" (Rom. 8:11). He has no regrets.

Knowledge gained outside of the Word of God would only make you zealous. Saul was full of zeal as he persecuted the followers of Christ. When Grace apprehended him and bestowed His Spirit upon him, the uncontrolled zeal of Saul became the consuming passion of Paul. Zeal is like "that which groweth of itself in the vineyard of knowledge and the grapes in it of thy vine undressed" (Lev. 25:11, in part).

Zeal is raw and uncontrolled and should not be deployed in that state. It could make a shipwreck of someone's destiny. When zeal is processed and channeled, it turns to a consuming and consummating passion for Christ. Zeal doesn't profit you, passion rewards you passionately.

"The grapes in it of thy vine undressed" are not good for the market. The grapes have to be processed. Your zeal has to be processed to become passion. Passion is profitable. The Psalmist says, the zeal of the Lord consumed me when they said let us go to the house of the Lord (Ps. 69:9).

Indeed, the tabernacle of God is the processing chamber for zeal. Romans 10:2 says, "For I bear them record that they have a zeal of God, but not according to knowledge."

A zeal for God is useless unless predicated upon knowledge of God. David with all the consuming zeal still had to go to the synagogue where the knowledge of God is acquired. "A wise man is strong; yea, a man of knowledge increaseth strength" (Prov. 24:5).

Knowledge is vital in your journey to gain understanding. Daniel understood by book. The disciples obtained knowledge through apprenticeship. They were with the Messiah. They saw, they observed—they were with the Son of God who mentored them. Peter was not of much education but learned by apprenticeship. Their knowledge base was fortified prior to their gaining understanding. God's instruction for you to get understanding is not without a reward. That divine call in Proverbs 4:7 carried a reward just like when you honor your parents.

Listen to God. "My son, eat thou honey, because it is good; and the honeycomb, which is sweet to thy taste: So shall the knowledge of wisdom be unto thy soul: when thou hast found it, then there shall be a reward, and thy expectation shall not be cut off" (Prov. 24:13–14).

The promise of a reward and the fulfillment of expectations, underscore the premium God placed over His word. However, knowledge is better comprehended and apprehended with experience. Truth is, that we have been comprehending principles without experiencing the love of God. We must grasp the experience of divine love. The experience of that love is what unites us as believers. It's our common experience without which there can be no understanding.

Seven things that happen when you read the Bible: (1) You enter into a relationship with The King and His Kingdom. (2) You access the instruction bank of The King and His Kingdom. (3) You acquire knowledge about The King and His Kingdom. (4) You communicate with The King on the basis of the knowledge acquired. (5) You confront Kingdom distractions. (6) You develop intimacy with God. (7) You enter into spiritual bonding with the Holy Spirit. These seven steps leading to spiritual understanding define the content of this book.

His Word first

When Jesus interjected Himself into the discussion of two of his disciples traveling to the village called Emmaus; He never wanted them to know Him through any other means than through the scripture. "And beginning from Moses and all the prophets, he expounded unto them in all the scriptures the things concerning himself" (Luke 24:27).

It is imperative that you know Him through His word before you touch Him. Revelation is precedent upon

GRACE IN HIS BOSOM

knowledge. God gave us His word first that we may get into His word. Until you get into His word, God cannot get His word into you.

Therefore get into God's word and God will get His word into you. When you get into logos, God will get rhema into you. In Jesus, God became a man that He can communicate directly with us. God as a spirit is separated from the sinful man. Jesus is called the Word of God because He came with a message. Jesus, the Word is God in human flesh and transforms those who believe in Him. God's primary purpose of pouring His word to us is to get us to believe that He is God-The Creator, Maker of heaven and earth, and a rewarder of those who diligently seek Him.

In the Book of Acts, the Ethiopian eunuch, after worship, still felt an intense yearning for God.

> And he arose and went: and, behold, a man of Ethiopia, an eunuch of great authority under Candace queen of the Ethiopians, who had the charge of all her treasure, and had come to Jerusalem for to worship, Was returning, and sitting in his chariot read Esaias the prophet. Then the Spirit said unto Philip, Go near, and join thyself to this chariot. And Philip ran thither to him, and heard him read the prophet Esaias, and said, Understandest thou what thou readest? And he said, How can I, except some man should guide me? And

he desired Philip that he would come up
and sit with him. (Acts 8:27–31)

The man of influence was returning from the Passover. He searched for God with all his heart. The annual convention didn't end his search. He was not satisfied with religion. After religious activities, your conversation should be more with the scriptures. You must come to Christ in faith, digging deeper to find. Most of us seek God but never search for Him.

The search in question is not the usual fishing expedition. The Ethiopian eunuch read from the same book Christ read in Luke 4:17. It was a logical search driven by seeking God and taking pain with vigor and fervency. In sincerity and uprightness, launch your whole heart in prayer. Those that seek him shall find Him. "And ye shall seek me, and find me, when ye shall search for me with all your heart" (Jer. 29:13).

Knowledge of the Bible

On June 27, 2008, while searching for materials on the subject of understanding, I was at a certain Christian bookstore at Mt. Kisco, New York. After a vigorous search of their stock without success, I asked the lady manager for help. She immediately pointed at a book directly opposite her. Excitedly, I picked up the text by Lee Strobel. I flipped through the contents in a hurry but couldn't find the word understanding.

I quickly reminded her that the book deal with the Darwinian Theory and so on. Yes, she responded. She added that the author of the book wasn't a Christian. He was a journalist who set out to investigate some Bible claims but ended up convicted and converted, she said. She quickly added that you can't read the Bible and remain the same.

Fixing her gaze at me, she declared, "If you are looking for understanding, read the Bible." I was startled. For a moment, I almost aborted this book project. Mary John was absolutely correct. Knowledge of the Bible is sine qua non to getting understanding.

Beyond that, it brought to mind the sensitive nature of that subject. Perhaps, that explains why many preachers believe that understanding spiritual understanding is un-teachable. Furthermore, it points to why there's a death of Christian literature on the subject of understanding.

Nonetheless, I was encouraged by the Holy Spirit which placed the assignment in my heart for over a decade. So it was that, whenever I tried to put pen on paper, I'd always hit a brick wall. Oftentimes I don't know where to start.

As I stood in that bookstore, that same spirit kept nudging me forward. I kept hearing, "Do not despair, do not give up. The whole essence of your assignment is to assist people to read the Bible." Those words emboldened me. I was convinced that God was about to use me to unveil the mystery surrounding spiritual understanding. Instantly, I realized that understanding is a process. It's only when knowledge is acquired about The King and His Kingdom that the basic requirements for understanding is fulfilled. Against that backdrop, I prayed for insight and God answered with revelation.

Divine intervention. When in the wee hours, the Holy Spirit dictated the content of this book to me, a generous measure of peace and boldness overcame me. Instantly, it dawned on me that the grace for the completion of the book was imparted to me. I sprang up to obey that voice that resonated beyond Habakkuk 2:2, "Write the vision and make it plain upon tables that he may run that readeth it." It was an open and direct vision. It needed no interpretation. Thereafter this book project became a pleasant journey. He that called me granted me the speed of accomplishment because faithful is He forever.

Study begets knowledge

Daniel 11:32 in part testify that "they that do know their God shall be strong and do exploits." Knowing God demands some sort of activities which are located in study and learning. God wants you to know Him via His Word. That's why He poured out Himself in His Word to you in the Bible.

Throughout the scripture, God continually appeals to you to study His Word. Truth is, there's no knowledge without study or learning. Study has a written-word domain as opposed to learning which may or may not depend entirely on letters.

You can learn how to drive a car without studying any driving manual but you can't study how to drive a car without going through the instruction manual.

The testimony of Daniel 11:32, came after Daniel "understood by books" (Dan. 9:2). Through study Daniel discovered what was said concerning the destiny of his people. With such an understanding, Daniel quickly gave attention to the Lord God. Knowledge is held captive by ignorance.

"My people are destroyed for lack of knowledge" (Obad. 1:17). Study liberate knowledge from the captivity of darkness. Every person's ignorance is his stronghold and knowledge is the light that shatters every darkness. That light is ignited in study. It is amazing that when you study, God can turn the light to explain the things that happen several years ago. If the gospel is hidden, it is indeed hidden to them that are lost. God created light before the sun. Light is in God's word. It is the Word (Gen. 1:1–11 and John 1:1). The entrance of the word giveth light, it giveth understanding unto the simple (Ps. 119:130).

God is relationship oriented based on the principle of His word. To receive from God, you must understand the word He spoke concerning you. You must understand His principles. You must obey Him based on His word. No one can set the rules for his relationship with God. Instructions from God become knowledge after you must have studied them.

Your strength as a believer is proportional to the knowledge of God which you acquired from studies. It is on the basis of such knowledge that you go to war to secure your glorious destiny in Christ. You become an overcomer when you do exploits. In all the miracles throughout the Bible, there are people who did something. They acted based on their knowledge of the promises of God concerning them or their generations.

Stressing that point, Apostle Paul says, "This charge I commit unto thee, son Timothy, according to the prophecies which went before on thee, that thou by them mightest war a good warfare" (1 Tim. 1:18). That book of the law did not depart from the mouth of Joshua day and night. He meditated upon what was written therein and was rewarded with good success (Josh. 1:8).

Against the foreground, Joshua declared boldly that "as for me and my household, we shall serve the LORD." You are only as strong as your knowledge base.

In 2 Chronicles 13:1–8, a challenge arose. Abijah confronted the challenge with boldness because of what he knew. Abijah knew from the written word that God gave the Kingdom to David and his sons by covenant of salt.

> And in the eighteenth year of king Jeroboam began Abijah to reign over Judah. He reigned three years in Jerusalem. His mother's name also was Michaiah the daughter of Uriel of Gibeah. And there was war between Abijah and Jeroboam. And Abijah set the battle in array with an army of valiant men of war, even four hundred thousand chosen men: Jeroboam also set the battle in array against him with eight hundred thousand chosen men, being mighty men of valour. And Abijah stood up upon mount Zemaraim, which

is in mount Ephraim, and said, Hear me, thou Jeroboam, and all Israel; Ought ye not to know that the LORD God of Israel gave the kingdom over Israel to David for ever, even to him and to his sons by a covenant of salt? Yet Jeroboam the son of Nebat, the servant of Solomon the son of David, is risen up, and hath rebelled against his lord. And there are gathered unto him vain men, the children of Belial, and have strengthened themselves against Rehoboam the son of Solomon, when Rehoboam was young and tenderhearted, and could not withstand them. And now ye think to withstand the kingdom of the LORD in the hand of the sons of David; and ye be a great multitude, and there are with you golden calves, which Jeroboam made you for gods.

Abijah was persuaded that God would never break His covenant or alter the things which had gone out of His mouth (Ps. 89:34).

David knew that the covenant God had with Israel was that of circumcision hence he went to war with it. Listen to David in 1 Samuel 17:26 (in part), "For who is this uncircumcised Philistine, that he should defy the armies of the living God?" What happened to Goliath after that declaration is forever an exciting Bible story. It is important that you "Study to show thyself approved unto God, a workman that needed not to be ashamed, rightly dividing the word of truth" (2 Tim. 2:15).

Again, to emphasize the importance of study, Paul told Timothy: "The cloke that I left at Troas with Carpus, when thou comest, bring with thee, and the books, but especially the parchments" (2 Tim. 4:13). Books and parchments are evidence of a heart that is seeking the Kingdom of God and its righteousness.

When you study the Bible you gain acquaintance with God. You recognize Him as the Almighty. Comprehension of that truth brings about familiarity. You are enlightened even as you receive insight. Your perceptive ability is sharpened such as you begin to receive and discern spiritual signals. "For God, who commanded the light to shine out of darkness, hath shined in our hearts, to give the light of the knowledge of the glory of God in the face of Jesus Christ" (2 Cor. 4:6).

The Word of God is the bearer of His light. The body of instruction received through study crystallizes into knowledge by the power that causes it to be. When God says be; it is a release of the power of what it causes you to be. "And God said, let there be light and there was light" (Gen. 1:3).

Instructively, God wants you to get serious with His word. Be sincere and committed to Christ. Listen to His desire for you as amplified in Hosea 6:4, 6. "O Ephraim, what shall I do unto thee? O Judah, what shall I do unto thee? for your goodness is as a morning cloud, and as the early dew it goeth away. For I desired mercy, and not sacrifice; and the knowledge of God more than burnt offerings."

God delights in loyalty and not sacrifice. Colossians 1:9–10 says, "For this cause we also, since the day we heard it, do not cease to pray for you, and to desire that ye might be filled with the knowledge of his will in all wisdom and spiritual understanding; That ye might walk worthy of the Lord unto all pleasing, being fruitful in every good work, and increasing in the knowledge of God."

Verse 10 highlighted three things that you must do: (1) Walk worthy of the Lord. (2) Become fruitful unto every good work. (3) Increasing the knowledge of God. Seeking to know God is a continuum. When you finish with the written word, God through the ministry of the Holy Spirit, will open the other book which was not written, known as revelation and the journey continues unto the perfect day (Prov. 4:18).

Isaiah 59:19 says, "So shall they fear the name of the LORD from the west, and his glory from the rising of the sun. When the enemy shall come in like a flood, the Spirit of the LORD shall lift up a standard against him." The Holy Spirit shall lift up a standard against the enemy. You may ask, what standard?

The standard that the Spirit of the LORD shall lift up resides in your knowledge. If your knowledge base is shallow, you have constrained the Holy Spirit per se. The Holy Spirit that indwells in you cannot manufacture any standard for you. He shall lift a standard commiserate with the standard you attained in the knowledge of God.

Knowledge is measured

In most nations, early education is measured in standard. You began from the lower standard and progressed accordingly. Similarly, in spiritual matters, knowledge is also measured. The scale of measurement ranges from milk to strong meat. Hebrews 5:12–14 puts it this way.

> For when for the time ye ought to be teachers, ye have need that one teach you again which be the first principles of the oracles of God; and are become such as have need of milk, and not of strong meat. For every one that useth milk is unskilful in the word of righteousness: for he is a babe. But strong meat belongeth to them that are of full age, even those who by reason of use have their senses exercised to discern both good and evil.

Milk is for babies and strong meat is for adults like you. However, between those two extremes are cheese and meat. Obviously, there are four levels of Kingdom knowledge notably: (1) milk standard, (2) cheese or solid milk standard, (3) meat standard, (4) strong meat standard. Interestingly, Ezekiel's account of the stream that flows from the temple depicts four levels of the knowledge of the Word of God. Listen to him.

> And when the man that had the line in his hand went forth eastward, he measured a thousand cubits, and he brought me through the waters; the waters were to the ancles. Again he measured a thousand, and brought me through the waters; the waters were to the knees. Again he measured a thousand, and brought me through; the waters were to the loins. Afterward he measured a thousand; and it was a river that I could not pass over: for the waters were risen, waters to swim in, a river that could not be passed over. (Ezek. 47:3–5)

In the above account, we got the following levels: (1) ankle level, (2) knee level, (3) waist level, (4) overflow level. Notice that at the first three levels, activities are restricted but at the overflow level, you are swimming and flowing with the current. At this level, you are at liberty to launch your boat, cast your net while Jesus will call in the harvest as He did for Simon.

The overflow is your divine destination. That's where God wants you to attain in His knowledge. It is the destination grace where things happen on their own accord. "And we know that all things work together for good to them that love God, to them who are the called according to his purpose" (Rom. 8:28). For that scripture to manifest in your life, you must attain the zone of love.

It's imperative that you strive to attain the highest standards such that when the devil shall come in like a flood, the Spirit of the Lord will find an appropriate standard to lift up against the enemy. Interestingly, the scripture says, "a standard." It is not the standard hence it is not uniform.

Glory to God, no one can define your standard but you. You got to sit down with the Book and read. The Bible is to be opened and read. It's neither a sartorial symbol of conformity nor a decorative item, to be strategically placed in your car, office table and anywhere else. The Word of God is to be autopaged in your heart.

Our Father is fervently appealing to you: "My son, eat thou honey, because it is good; and the honeycomb which is sweet to thy taste" (Prov. 24:23). Indeed, the Word of God is good and sweet. Like the honey, chew, lick and swallow it raw. It will not only nourish you but like the lamp, that it is; direct your path to your glorious destiny in Christ.

Knowledge before worship. Knowledge and power which coalesced on the day of Pentecost find expression in worship. In Luke 24:13–32,

> Jesus opened their eyes via the written word and they knew Him. "And, behold, two of them went that same day to a village called Emmaus, which was from Jerusalem about threescore furlongs. And they talked together of all these things which had happened. And it came to pass, that, while they communed together and reasoned, Jesus himself drew near,

GRACE IN HIS BOSOM

and went with them. But their eyes were holden that they should not know him. And he said unto them, What manner of communications are these that ye have one to another, as ye walk, and are sad? And the one of them, whose name was Cleopas, answering said unto him, Art thou only a stranger in Jerusalem, and hast not known the things which are come to pass there in these days? And he said unto them, What things? And they said unto him, Concerning Jesus of Nazareth, which was a prophet mighty in deed and word before God and all the people: And how the chief priests and our rulers delivered him to be condemned to death, and have crucified him. But we trusted that it had been he which should have redeemed Israel: and beside all this, to day is the third day since these things were done. Yea, and certain women also of our company made us astonished, which were early at the sepulchre; And when they found not his body, they came, saying, that they had also seen a vision of angels, which said that he was alive. And certain of them which were with us went to the sepulchre, and found it even so as the women had said: but him they saw not. Then he said unto them, O fools, and slow of heart to believe all that the prophets have spoken: Ought not Christ to have suffered these things, and to enter into his glory? And beginning at Moses and all the prophets, he expounded unto them in all the scriptures the things concerning himself. And they drew nigh unto the village, whither they went: and he made as though he would have gone further. But they constrained him, saying, Abide with us: for it is toward evening, and the day is far spent. And he went in to tarry with them. And it came to pass, as he sat at meat with them, he took bread, and blessed it, and brake, and gave to them. And their eyes were opened, and they knew him; and he vanished out of their sight. And they said one to another, Did not our heart burn within us, while he talked with us by the way, and while he opened to us the scriptures?"

They knew Jesus through the scriptures before they worshiped Him. Proverbs 2:1–2 says, "My son, if thou wilt receive my words, and hide my commandments with thee; So that thou incline thine ear unto wisdom, and apply thine heart to understanding."

Receiving the word first is indeed a Kingdom priority. The synergy between knowledge, wisdom, understanding, and power is progressive. (1) Study provokes knowledge. (2) Knowledge provokes wisdom. (3) Wisdom provokes intimacy. (4) Intimacy provokes understanding. (5) Understanding provokes worship. (6) Worship provokes power. No worship, no power. You can have all the knowledge; without worship you are powerless. Power is released on the platform of worship.

It's the intention of God that you know Him through His word. You can't worship a God you don't know. Worship must spring from your knowledge of God.

In worship, you entreat God; you beseech Him; you honor and glorify Him. You cannot do any of those things without availing yourself of His way and principles. Should you decide to worship without knowledge you run the prospect of traveling the way of Job.

Knowledge with worship. Worship is important to God. He created us to worship him. Worship is the major assignment of the angels in heaven. "And all the angels stood round about the throne, and about the elders and the four beasts, and fell before the throne on their faces, and worshipped God, Saying, Amen: Blessing, and glory, and wisdom, and thanksgiving, and honour, and power, and might, be unto our God for ever and ever. Amen" (Rev. 7:11–12).

God's desire is for you to seek and worship Him. Consequently, the knowledge of God must not be without worship. The man of Ezekiel 47 measured four times at equal intervals of 560 yards with his scale. At each interval (ankles, knees, loins, and deepest levels) I perceive that he must have installed a peg, pillar, or beacon.

The significance of spiritual markers is huge. No matter the level of the knowledge of God that you attain, worship must accompany it in direct proportion. At each level, the beacon is symbolic of an altar. The altar as your place of worship is also your place of commitment.

Your knowledge of God is directly proportional to your worship of Him. No knowledge, no worship. Less knowledge, less worship. More knowledge, more worship. If the knowledge of God is without worship, it is nothing but an academic exercise.

You can study Bible knowledge in college without knowing God. You may be religious yet lost. That's not the type of knowledge that God is trusting you to acquire. In God's divine agenda or plan, worship is an integral part of knowledge and in direct proportion.

When God revealed Himself to Abram, he built an altar (Gen. 12:7). Jacob anointed the pillar (Gen. 31:13). Any knowledge of God that discards worship is one not to be pursued. Seeking to know God must be in worship. You worship God with your time, treasure, and talents.

The many times God sent Moses to Pharaoh, the common refrain was the same: Let my people go that they may serve me (Exod. 7:16, 8:1, 8:20, 9:1, 9:13, 10:3). Why would God put the nation and people of Egypt under severe torment if the issue of worship was not a Kingdom priority?

Worship is a serious Kingdom issue. At the end of the measurement, the man of Ezekiel 47:6 said unto Ezekiel, "Son of man, hast thou seen this?" The Good News translation puts it this way. "Mortal man, note all this carefully." That statement underpins the importance God puts on the synergy of Kingdom knowledge and worship.

In the scripture, water is symbolic of the Word of God. The water flowing out from the threshold of the temple is indeed the Word of God gushing out from the source— the Holy of Holies. At whatever level you advanced in the knowledge of God, you are expected to place a pillar. Pillars are landmarks. They are beacons. The beacon becomes your commitment to worship.

However, at the fourth and final level, you are doing exploits for worship is your way of life. You are now an overcomer.

Aroma of knowledge

The aroma of knowledge is the unique anointing that is available through worship. You may earn a PhD in Christian religious education, but without worship, you cannot contact the aroma of knowledge.

The story of the woman with the alabaster box is forever intriguing. Each time I read that story some sort of sensation runs through my spine. Ointments are never packaged to be broken. They have covers or corks that are designed to permit a guided discharge of the contents. The woman would have easily and gently opened the guard to drop the ointments on Jesus.

She chose to break it and empty the contents on Jesus. "And being in Bethany in the house of Simon the leper, as he sat at meat, there came a woman having an alabaster box of ointment of spikenard very precious; and she brake the box, and poured it on his head" (Mark 14:3).

John 12:3 put it this way. "Then took Mary a pound of ointment of spikenard, very costly, and anointed the feet of Jesus, and wiped his feet with her hair: and the house was filled with the odour of the ointment." The woman worshipped with her most precious treasure. She broke the ointment and poured it; thereby anointed Jesus. As if that was not enough, she wiped the feet with her hair.

Everything Mary did was out of the ordinary. Indeed, her actions were a demonstration of Kingdom violence similar to that Jesus spoke about in Matthew 11:12. In the process, she contacted the anointing. The scripture recorded that the sweet aroma of the perfume ventilated the house. When that happened, the aroma of the knowledge of Jesus went out.

First, it followed Mary home because she used her hair to wipe his feet. Beyond that, the prevailing wind which ventilated the house ensures that you contacted the anointing. "The wind bloweth where it listeth, and thou hearest the sound thereof, but canst not tell whence it cometh, and whither it goeth: so is every one that is born of the Spirit" (John 3:8).

So long you are born of the Spirit, you contacted the anointing and the aroma of the knowledge of God manifested through you. The wind is still available.

> Now thanks be unto God, which always causeth us to triumph in Christ, and maketh manifest the savour of his knowledge by us in every place. For we are unto God a sweet savour of Christ, in them

that are saved, and in them that perish: To
the one we are the savour of death unto
death; and to the other the savour of life
unto life. And who is sufficient for these
things? (2 Cor. 2:14–16)

If you are born again, you contacted the sweet-smelling fragrance of the knowledge of Jesus Christ. That's why God is using you to spread the knowledge everywhere. Jesus released the power that causes it to be as soon as He understood the indignation of His disciples concerning that woman's act.

Expressly, He gave a restraining order: "Leave her alone." What Jesus said next crystallizes the relationship between that aromatic anointing and the knowledge of the gospel. "Verily I say unto you, Wheresoever this gospel shall be preached in the whole world, there shall also this, that this woman hath done, be told for a memorial of her" (Matt. 26:13).

Now, you can understand the divine link between the fragrance and the knowledge of God and most importantly, why the power that causes it to be was released through you like a sweet-smelling fragrance. You are a sweet savor of Christ. Savor is the same as aroma. When you step out, understand that you are the sweet aroma of Christ.

Praise in knowledge. Heaven is the seat of God. He has the earth as His footstool. Praise defines the heavenly environment. If you desire that God should intervene in your situation, you must enact His divine environment over you. That divine environment is praise. David was a praise warrior. Praise is consequent upon knowledge.

In Psalms 119:171, David says, "My lips shall utter praise, when thou hast taught me thy statutes." You don't learn how to praise. It instinctively manifests from the inside of you. Simply open your mouth and pay the sacrifice of your lips. "By him therefore let us offer the sacrifice of praise to God continually, that is, the fruit of our lips giving thanks to his name" (Heb. 13:15). When God descends in the midst of your praises, He will tabernacle with you. He will covenant with you. You will build Him an altar where He met you. That altar will remain your place of commitment. The altar that ventilates your sacrifice will answer for you.

Neither sin nor praise. In all his tribulation, Job didn't sin with his lips. "But he said unto her, Thou speakest as one of the foolish women speaketh. What? shall we receive good at the hand of God, and shall we not receive evil? In all this did not Job sin with his lips" (Job 2:10). In the same token, he didn't praise with his lips. Convinced of his own innocence, Job engaged in lamentation, justified himself and blamed God. He rumbled enough to earn the wrath of Elihu, the younger bystander who showed knowledge and wisdom. Elihu clearly knew his God. No ambiguity about that.

Revelation knowledge

In a nutshell, revelation is the word that you "saw." It is the other Bible that was never printed. It was not meant to be for everyone. Revelation knowledge is so personal such that God speaks directly to the heart of His elect. Put differently the Holy Spirit, the same Spirit that indwells in man, speaks from the inner recesses of man.

From the beginning, God requested you to hide His word in your heart. When His word begin to jump out of your heart and you behold them in your eyes, that's when you arrive at your point of revelation. It is simply the word that you behold in your eyes. The threshold of revelation is your heart-that incubator and innermost recesses of man.

Listen to Isaiah 1:1.

> The vision of Isaiah the son of Amoz, which he saw concerning Judah and Jerusalem in the days of Uzziah, Jotham, Ahaz, and Hezekiah, kings of Judah.
>
> Revelation is often picture and motion based. It is the video clips you behold concerning the destiny of anything. The script is written in your heart and motions towards your sensory organs of cognition. In the scripture above, notice that Isaiah saw the vision. Vision in itself is a complete package. It may come to you in clips or slides depending on how God purposes that you should receive it. The bottomline was that Isaiah saw it. The great prophet watched the video. Again, he saw another. Again the word that Isaiah

the son of Amoz saw concerning Judah
and Jerusalem. (Isa. 2:1)

The last book of the Bible is known as revelation. It was "The Revelation of Jesus Christ, which God gave unto him, to shew unto his servants things which must shortly come to pass; and he sent and signified it by his angel unto his servant John: Who bare record of the Word of God, and of the testimony of Jesus Christ, and of all things that he saw" (Rev. 1:1–2).

It is obvious from the passages above, that everything about revelation was revealed and they included (1) that the Source of revelation is Jesus Christ—the Living Word. (2) That revelation is given (released) (3) That the recipients have intimate relationships with God. (4) Revelation is futuristic. (5) That the revealed have absolute chance of occurrence. (6) Angels have a part to play. (7) The recipients must be couriers of The Good News. (8) Revelation is received via the sensory organ of sight.

The Kingdom

In Matthew 6:33, Jesus declared, "But seek ye first His Kingdom and His righteousness, and all these things will be given to you as well." Kingdom citizenship is very important to God. Everything you desire is made available on the platform of your being a bona fide member of His Kingdom on earth. It's erroneous to assume that Kingdom citizenship is automatic. Salvation is free, Kingdom citizenship is by choice. It's by aspiration. Jesus says you should seek first His kingdom.

Put differently, you must aspire to be a member. God gave you the power of choice. He expects that you should make great and wise choices. Choosing to belong to His kingdom community on earth rank uppermost on the scale of choices. Many times Jesus spoke about the Kingdom.

The kingdom is the bedrock of every relationship that we have on earth. It defines the whole range of our common experience in Christ hence you must be a Kingdom citizen to behold the kingdom experience.

Membership of the Kingdom. Qualification for membership of the Kingdom of God is simple: receive Jesus— the Word, the Living Word. As soon as you receive God's Word by confessing Christ as your Lord and Savior, the investiture as a Kingdom citizen is automatically conferred on you by the governor of the earth-The Holy Spirit.

God expects that every member of the Kingdom community must as a matter of priority understand the culture and fundamental principles of the Kingdom.

The kingdom has values, laws, morals, lifestyles, language, and strategic interests. Also the kingdom has one common enemy variously referred to as satan, devil, adversary, the prince of the world.

Knowledge of the Kingdom culture and way of life deliver a two-fold result. First, it enables you to maintain a right—standing before the King of kings and the Lord of lords. Also, it's the antidote to the devices of the enemy. However, the most impactful effect is that it provides a common field of experience for every Kingdom citizen.

Sharing in the Kingdom

Being a Kingdom citizen is not enough. You must share in the common field of experience. The commonality of the field of experience is located in Christ. Jesus Christ epitomizes your experience as a Kingdom citizen. You were admitted into the kingdom through Him. To be born again, you must confess Christ as your Lord and Savior. That's the pathway.

Amplifying that in John 14:6, "Jesus saith unto him, I am the way, the truth, and the life: no man cometh unto the Father, but by me." God gave that we may share Christ in Him and Him in Christ. The kernel of the gift of Christ is that we may share. "For God so loved the world, that he gave his only begotten Son, that whosoever believeth in him should not perish, but have everlasting life" (John 3:16). God values relationships.

Understanding is key to every successful relationship. Understanding delivers dividends. Perspective is the dividend of understanding. Perspective is everything. Perspective is how you see everything. Here's the Kingdom mindset: "I know both how to be abased, and I know how to abound: everywhere and in all things I am instructed both to be full and to be hungry, both to abound and to suffer need. I can do all things through Christ which strengtheneth me" (Phil. 4:12–13).

Sharing promotes intimacy. Intimacy is a necessary requirement for understanding. It is not possible to achieve intimacy, without sharing. It is the quest to learn more of each other; to share out of the commonality of the field of experience, that understanding is wrought. As a Kingdom citizen, Christ is in you and He is greater than the enemy that is in the world. "Ye are of God, little children, and have overcome them: because greater is he that is in you, than he that is in the world" (1 John 4:4).

Christ commissioned you to go to the four corners of the earth and share Him with others. As a Kingdom citizen, you are on a redemptive mission with Jesus to the ends of the earth. I don't know how many people you have shared Christ with. It is important that you get your world settled about one thing: the Kingdom is all about sharing. If you are not sharing, you are not living the Kingdom experience. How many souls have you led to Christ? There's joy in heaven when a soul is saved.

God gave hence you must give. "Give, and it shall be given unto you; good measure, pressed down, and shaken together, and running over, shall men give into your bosom. For with the same measure that ye mete withal it shall be measured to you again" (Luke 6:38). The scripture above encapsulates the Kingdom experience. If you believe so, you must have come to the place of the people of 1 Peter 3:8–10,

> Finally, be ye all of one mind, having compassion one of another, love as brethren, be pitiful, be courteous: Not rendering evil for evil, or railing for railing: but contrariwise blessing; knowing that ye are thereunto called, that ye should inherit a blessing. For he that will love life, and see

HENRY A. FAGBOLA

good days, let him refrain his tongue from evil, and his lips that they speak no guile.

In his second address to the people of Corinth, Apostle Paul said inter alia:

> But this I say, He which soweth sparingly shall reap also sparingly; and he which soweth bountifully shall reap also bountifully. Every man according as he purposeth in his heart, so let him give; not grudgingly, or of necessity: for God loveth a cheerful giver. And God is able to make all grace abound toward you; that ye, always having all sufficiency in all things, may abound to every good work: (As it is written, He hath dispersed abroad; he hath given to the poor: his righteousness remaineth for ever. Now he that ministereth seed to the sower both minister bread for your food, and multiply your seed sown, and increase the fruits of your righteousness;) Being enriched in every thing to all bountifulness, which causeth through us thanksgiving to God. For the administration of this service not only supplieth the want of the saints, but is abundant also by many thanksgivings unto God; Whiles by the experiment of this ministration they glorify God for your professed subjection

unto the gospel of Christ, and for your liberal distribution unto them, and unto all men; And by their prayer for you, which long after you for the exceeding grace of God in you. Thanks be unto God for his unspeakable gift. (2 Cor. 9:6–15)

Sharing and generosity is a gift and the key to Kingdom prosperity. Your kingdom sharing makes available in abundance, the unique opportunities for many thanksgiving.

Kingdom values and culture

Here are some of the Kingdom values and culture which every Kingdom citizen must comprehend. Knowledge of these may be acquired simultaneously or sequentially. They include baptism, love, believe, faith, hope, receive, joy, obedience, integrity, given, confession, language, commitment, forgiveness, temperance, humility, patience, boldness, longsuffering, worship, sanctification, prayer, praise.

Love. Prior to Jesus's declaration in Matthew 6:33, God was fed up with watching you trying without success to obtain the things of the Kingdom without a love relationship with the King. Without hesitation, Jesus stated the priority of the Kingdom and the pathway to obtain the same. Simply put, Jesus says, (a) strive to become a kingdom citizen, (b) strive to relate favorably with the King, and (c) all the things that you scramble for are predicated upon those two divine dimensions: His kingdom and His righteousness.

Expressly, God calls you to a love relationship. He did so because his character is love. His banner over you is love. God is majestically attired in love. When asked what was the greatest commandment, Jesus's response was wrapped in love: "Love God and obey Him. Love your neighbor as yourself." Love means so much to God. It is all about sacrifice. Love revolves around giving. Put differently, giving is the fulcrum upon which love revolves. "For God so loved the world that he gave his only begotten son that whosoever believe might have everlasting life" (John 3:16). He so love the world that He sacrificed his Son Jesus on the altar of salvation.

Consequently you cannot love without giving. You must give the gift of self. Sacrifice is central to God's agenda concerning you. So long the earth remains, seed time and harvest time will never cease. Granted, God can substitute your seed as he did for Abraham. He can collapse time to bless you as He did for Nehemiah. The only thing God never did was to abolish sacrifice. Sacrifice is absolute and constant. Irrespective of the season and the premium placed on your seed, sowing must be accomplished. Time and seed are variables while sowing remains constant.

Calling on God depends largely on your belief. God values relationships. Conversation is the bedrock of relationships of a righteous Father with His sons. It would be difficult for anyone to call on a father he does not believe in. Calling on God is to be preceded by believe. Believe is preceded by hearing the Word of God. Expectedly, faith is encapsulated in your belief. The sequence is simple. Believe first, thereafter exercise faith. Believe comes before faith. Faith is to be exercised in the direction of your belief. Your faith is fastened to your belief.

Baptism

Then cometh Jesus from Galilee to Jordan unto John, to be baptized of him. But John forbad him, saying, I have need to be baptized of thee, and comest thou to me? And Jesus answering said unto him, Suffer it to be so now: for thus it becometh us to fulfil all righteousness. Then he suffered him. (Matt. 3:13–15)

Baptism was the first public act that Jesus submitted Himself to. Also, the same ushers the earlier events of His earthly ministry. In His last statement before ascension, Jesus commanded the church to, among other things, baptize new converts as a matter of priority. The significance of the ordinance of baptism can't be lost on believers. Essentially, baptism is an important part of the Great Commission. Baptism is largely misunderstood; hence, it is regarded as a dangerous subject among church groups. The conflict arises as to the *how* of baptism rather than the *why*.

In this essay, we're concerned about the *why*. The *why* provides the reason why Jesus rebuked John from dissuading Him to partake of that all-important ordinance. In baptism, Christ shared with every believer His priesthood, His death, His burial, and His resurrection. Without a sharing in the common experience in Christ, spiritual understanding becomes a distant possibility. Drawing from that perspective, we discover the following:

a. (a) Baptism must follow repentance. "If ye keep my commandments, ye shall abide in my

love; even as I have kept my Father's commandments, and abide in his love" (John 15:10).

b. Baptism identifies you with Christ. "For as many of you as have been baptized into Christ have put on Christ" (Gal. 3:27).

c. Baptism is a portrayal of the death, burial, and resurrection of Jesus.

Know ye not, that so many of us as were baptized into Jesus Christ were baptized into his death? Therefore we are buried with him by baptism into death: that like as Christ was raised up from the dead by the glory of the Father, even so we also should walk in newness of life. For if we have been planted together in the likeness of his death, we shall be also in the likeness of his resurrection: Knowing this, that our old man is crucified with him, that the body of sin might be destroyed, that henceforth we should not serve sin. (Rom. 6:3–6).

d. (The desire among the saved is to die to self and to live in Christ. In a nutshell, baptism is following Jesus as well as obeying Christ.

"And Jesus came and spake unto them, saying, All power is given unto me in heaven and in earth. Go ye there-fore, and teach all nations, baptizing them in the name of the Father, and of the Son, and of the Holy Ghost: Teaching them to observe all things whatsoever I have commanded you: and, lo, I am with you always, even unto the end of the world. Amen. (Matt. 28:18–20)

GRACE IN HIS BOSOM

Also, baptism is a public identification with Jesus as in Acts 2:41, "Then they that gladly received his word were baptized: and the same day there were added unto them about three thousand souls."

Nonetheless, the baptism that unites us is by the Spirit. It involves every believer and takes place at salvation.

"But ye are not in the flesh, but in the Spirit, if so be that the Spirit of God dwell in you. Now if any man have not the Spirit of Christ, he is none of his." (Rom. 8:9).

Believe. There are two scriptures that made me immensely aware of the practical impersonal nature of our relationship with God. First is, Jeremiah 33:3 which says, "Call unto me and I will answer you and show you great and mighty things which you do not know." Each time I call in obedience, directing my desire to the One who asked me to do so, the response has always been practical and immediate. Jeremiah 33:3 brought Jesus so close to me such that I needed no one to convince me about the efficacy of the Word of God. Jeremiah 33:3 is the master card in my evangelism kit. Whenever I notice that someone is confused and restless; that's my caveat emptor. With the most compassionate tune, I will release that hotline, pleading with the individual to prove him now. Just call I would enthuse. The result has always been amazing. God always answer in the most practical and personal manner.

The second scripture is (1 Peter 4:4, in part), "Greater is he that is in me than he that is in the world." This scripture is my kingdom anthem. The scripture is automatically programmed in my heart. It has become my daily refrain. I cannot recount how many times that I confess the scripture daily. Consciously or otherwise, he that is in me remained greater than he that is in the world. How amazing is the Word of God. Against that backdrop, it was a pleasant surprise as I listened to the interrogation of Jeremiah 33 verse 3 by belief and company in Romans 10:14. Listen carefully. "How then shall they call on him in whom they have not believed and how shall they believe in him of whom they have not heard? and how shall they hear without a preacher?"

As I reversed that scripture, my evangelism modus operandi came to mind. My approach seem to fit into the structure canvassed by Romans 10:14, which summarizes as follows: (1) Listen to the preacher. (2) Receive the good news. (3) Believe the good news. (4) Call the king of kings.

Most importantly that scripture is yet another proof that unbelieve is a major killer of the Kingdom community. Everything you desire, will answer to your belief. Trust is a subset of belief. Faith is fastened to your belief. It is to be exercised in the direction of your belief. Calling on God is consequent upon your belief. God values relationships. Communication is the bedrock of relationship. It would be difficult for anyone to initiate conversation with a father he does not trust. Intimate relationships is a function of trust. You must intentionally stay in communication with him.

The first public statement of Jesus Christ after he returned from the wilderness buttressed the importance of belief. Hear Him. "And saying, the time is fulfilled, and the kingdom of God is at hand: repent ye, and believe the gospel" (Mark 1:15).

GRACE IN HIS BOSOM

Faith must be in something before it works. Your faith resonates in your belief. "For God so loved the world, that he gave his only begotten Son, that whosoever believed in him should not perish but have eternal life" (John 3:16). Jesus completed the work. What to do is to believe. When you pray, believe that you receive (Mark 11:22–24).

Faith. Faith and belief are interwoven. They are like Siamese twins. It is difficult to separate them. Faith is an important Kingdom value. The definition of faith in Hebrews 11:1 is self-explanatory." Now faith is the substance of things hoped for, the evidence of things not seen. "Faith demands action. It remains passive until you activate it. "But without faith it is impossible to please him: for he that cometh to God must believe that he is and that he is a rewarder of them that diligently seek him" (Heb. 11:6).

Oftentimes, when analyzing the definition of faith, as portrayed in Hebrews 11:1; most preachers pay attention to substance, hope and evidence. No doubt all three are vital to the subject of faith. However, the secret of faith operation is located in the three letter word NOW. For belief to be sustained, faith must run like current, never ceasing, but drawing constantly from the element of immediacy. Timeliness, not size accounts for the dynamism of faith—operation.

Now is the deadline of faith. The subject of faith in all shades (faithful, faithfully, faithfulness) was used 356 times in the Bible. At new birth, you are given the measure of faith. That measure of faith is to be exercised in daily dosage. Call it one-a-day faith. You can neither exhaust nor deflate that measure of faith. It can remain dormant if you choose not to be proactive. Bless God that the now-moment is never in short supply. It is the current. Now is that opportunity that every believer craves for. Incidentally, when it comes many are incapable of identifying it because it is hidden in a three-letter word. God uses the simple to confound the wise.

Now is contacting the anointing; for what gets in the head, gets in the body. Now is a gift. It is the simplest of all gifts. You can neither feel it nor touch it but it follows you everywhere. Now is a gift, in the sense that opportunity is a gift. Opportunity to bless someone is a gift, for in it is your liberty and prosperity. Every opportunity is a challenge.

Now is going forth. Psalms 126:6 says, "He that goeth forth and weepeth, bearing precious seed, shall doubtless come again with rejoicing, bringing his sheaves with him." Your seed does not qualify to be called precious until it goes forth and exerts some burden on you. You must deal with such a struggle. The atmosphere for the miraculous comes in the now-moment.

In Genesis 22:7–8,

> And Isaac spake unto Abraham his father, and said, My father; and he said, Here I am, my son. And he said, behold the fire and the wood: but where is the lamb for the burnt offering? And Abraham said, My son, God will provide himself a lamb for a burnt offering: so they went both of them together.

GRACE IN HIS BOSOM

At that point, Abraham was convinced that even if he sacrificed Isaac, God will raise up another Isaac for him. To get to the point "God will" you must, as a matter of priority put aside the mind. Reason is no longer required, only God will. It is a transition that must crucify doubt on the altar of God's willingness.

For the three Hebrew lads in Daniel 3:17–18 (Shedrack, Meshach, and Abednego) it was a transition from His ability to willingness. Hear them: "If it be so, our God whom we serve is able to deliver us from the burning fiery furnace, and he will deliver us out of thine hand, o king. But if not, be it known unto thee, o king, that we will not serve thy gods nor worship the golden image which thou hast set up." These Hebrew kids got to the point of, "if I perish let me perish." People that often get to that point in the theater of their belief, never perish. Your desires are at the mercy of your declarations.

Now His will. The wedding in Cana Galilee as recorded in John 2:1–10, Mary demonstrated both the now strategy and the declaration of His willingness. Jesus literally told Mary, step aside woman and leave me alone, for I am but a mere observer here. Nonetheless, Mary ignored God to give birth to the miraculous ministry of Jesus. Indeed Mary delivered the second time.

Recall that; Mary gave birth to God in human flesh. Again she midwifed the miraculous ministry of Jesus. How was that possible? Mary's unyielding faith forced out (purchased) the first miracle of Jesus. In response to Jesus "my hour is not yet come,"

I perceive that Mary must have said; Son I know you. Your ability is never in doubt. I am convinced you will do it here and now. For this is the place and now the moment. I plead with you to read that passage carefully and you will notice that the word now played a role. That was not accidental.

In the Good News Bible translation, the word now occurs three times. Now began the process. Now refined it and now distilled it. When Mary told the disciples "whatsoever he asked you to do, do it," at that decisive moment, Jesus could no longer contain the miracle. He was in a hurry to discharge hence he gave a command to the servants, "Fill these jars with water." That command would startle you: "Now draw....; which now...had turned...; But until now!"

Listen, folk, if you confess His willingness in the now moment, it doesn't matter if you are undeserving or not, God will honor your faith. When these conditions are in place, God honors your faith even when it is ill-motivated. It never bothered Jesus that those vessels (six water pots) were filthy.

God can use you irrespective of your prevailing circumstances or conditions. What matters to God is that He looked around and found in you a vessel worthy for His use. Those six water pots were after the order of the purification of the Jews. They were holding water used for performing ablation—water for washing of feet, hands, and face plus head before prayer. The prevailing uncomfortable atmosphere could no longer constrain the miraculous because Mary had fulfilled the condition.

Now is the exercise of the covenant. It is the secret of faith operation. It is the deadline that ushers in the miraculous. You may feel like a spectator in the household of God but in God's agenda, you are the star of the now-moment. You are not seemingly that dirty vessel but the center of attraction. Therefore, your story will reveal the glory of God. People will see you and believe.

God's ability is never in doubt. Nevertheless, His willingness has to be confessed. Mary understood that and declared it in the now moment and necessitated the first miracle of Jesus. You too can do the same now. Your miracle is at your beck and call. Faith it in or faith it out now.

The issue of faith has taken such a space because it is vitally important. Faith in the Kingdom is like money matters. You must grasp that now.

Release of power

In the arena of the spirit, the release of power is precedent upon your eagerness to bring the willingness of God to bear on your situation. As soon as you do that, you will understand how pleasant it is for God to intervene.

The good news is that Jesus always says, I will. It is God's I will that releases the power of what it causes it to be. The power resonates in His willingness and not in His ability.

God's ability is wrapped up in covenants. Ephesians 4:20 puts it this way. "Now to him that is able to do far more abundantly beyond all that we ask or think, according to the power that works within us." God's ability to intervene in your situation is at the mercy of the power that works within you.

The power that works within you is located in your confession. You must open your mouth and vocalize; Lord I know you will do it. As soon as that is concluded and you believe it, a release of what it causes it to be, depart heaven.

The "now unto him" of Ephesians 4:20, implies a covenant relationship. It simply means covenant unto Him. Abraham understood that he was in covenant such that when Isaac demanded to know the seed to be sowed (Gen. 22:7–8), Abraham responded: "God himself will provide one." In Genesis 22:12–13, a release departed heaven in a blaze of glory and reached earth as a ram. That release, that ram was transported on the wings of Abraham's confessing the willingness of God. That's why it located Abraham at that place and moment. The Word of God is spoken to be spoken.

In Matthew 8:2–3,

> And behold there came a leper and worshiped him saying, Lord, if thou wilt, thou canst make me clean. And Jesus put forth his, hand and touched him, saying, I will; be thou clean. And immediately his leprosy was cleansed." Also, "And when Jesus was entered into Capernaum, there came unto him a centurion, beseeching him, And saying, Lord, my servant lieth at home sick of the palsy, grievously tor-

mented. And Jesus saith unto him, I will come and heal him.

"The Spirit indeed is willing, but the flesh is weak" (Matt. 26:41). God is Spirit and they that worship Him must do so in Spirit and in truth. The flesh represents the thought process of man that runs contrary to the Word of God. God's willingness is located in His word. Therefore confess His word. God is so obsessed with blessing you to the extent that He ignored the suffering of His begotten Son, Jesus in His most agonizing moment. At the garden of Gethsemane, Jesus pleaded with God even cautiously, that He might abort the journey to Calvary and the impending supreme sacrifice but God permitted His will to prevail.

In Genesis 1:28, God blessed you. "He charged you to be fruitful, and multiply, and replenish the earth, and subdue it: and have dominion over the fish of the sea, and over the fowl of the air, and over every living thing that moveth upon the earth."

Consequently, God could not watch the enemy wreck havoc on you, the bearer of His blessing. He was willing to sacrifice His only begotten Son in order to rescue you from any form of pain and hardship. God's willingness to intervene in your issues or circumstances find expression in His blessing of Genesis 1:28. God can't deny Himself. He is not a man that He should lie neither the son of man that He should repent (Num. 23:19–20).

"Every good gift and every perfect gift is from above, and cometh down from the Father of lights, with whom is no variableness, neither shadow of turning" (James 1:17).

Those words that went forth in Genesis 1:28, were wrapped in the willingness of God. The earth, He gave to you to dominate. God doesn't contradict Himself. His promises in Him are yea and in Him amen, unto the glory of God by us (2 Cor. 1:20).

The love of God found you right where you were hiding. His love is the conveyor of His willingness hence His compassion fail not. They are new every day (Lam. 3:22–23).

Jesus never ignored any cry for mercy because He was continually filled with passion. The cry for mercy from two blind men who sat by the road halted momentarily His journey to Jerusalem. Listen to them: "Have mercy on us, O Lord, thou son of David" (Matt. 20:30). In response, "Jesus stood still and called them and said, what will ye that I shall do unto you? They say unto him, Lord, that our eyes may be opened. So Jesus had compassion on them, and touched their eyes; and immediately their eyes received sight, and they followed him" (Matt. 20:32–34).

Obviously, Jesus knew they were blind. He could go ahead and heal their sight but He withheld the healing miracle until they confessed His willingness.

Permit me to draw similarity between the response of Jesus at this instance to that He offered to Mary at the wedding in the Cana of Galilee. "Jesus saith unto her, woman, what have I to do with thee? mine hour is not yet come" (John 2:4). Jesus could not act until his mother confessed his willingness by saying unto the servants, "whatsoever he saith unto you do it." After that the miracle began.

Thank God that he gave you a mouth and wisdom. Open your mouth wide just like the blind men who could not be silenced by the intimidating crowd. That is a sure way to secure your breakthrough. When your hour comes, you are no longer concerned with the person next to you. You are completely sowed in worship to Him who created you.

Call now. Whenever life seems to have converged on you and it appears you have missed the trajectory of your glorious destiny. The simple thing to do is to get back to God. Jesus will come and get you and reposition you. God has one purpose but many plans. They are plans of good and not evil, to give you the expected end.

> For I know the thoughts that I think towards you, saith the LORD, thoughts of peace, and not of evil, to give you an expected end. Then shall ye call upon me and ye shall go and pray unto me, and I will hearken unto you. And ye shall seek me and find me when you shall search for me with all your heart. And I will be found of you, saith the LORD: and I will turn away your captivity, and I will gather you from all the nations and from all the places whither I have driven you again into the place whence I caused you to be carried away captive. (Jer. 29:11–14)

Notice the abundance of "I will" in verse 14. That's very significant and suggestive that whenever you mess up with one plan, God will pull out another; so long you get back to Him. Nevertheless, the heart of man is desperately wicked, who can tell (Jer. 17:9). Jesus knew all men and did not commit Himself to them (John 2:24).

The Collapse of Time

"Behold, the days come, saith the LORD, that the plowman shall overtake the reaper, and the treader of grapes him that soweth seed; and the mountains shall drop sweet wine, and all the hills shall melt" (Amos 9:13). The Good News translation put it this way: "The days are coming says the LORD, When grain will grow faster than it can be harvested, and grapes will grow faster than the wine can be made. The mountains will drip with sweet wine and the hills will flow with it."

Today, that scripture is fulfilled to your hearing. God has literally compressed time or taken it out of the equation. It is now seed-harvest. The old order of long wait may no longer prevail in your situation.

God can collapse time to bless you as He did in the case of Hezekiah (2 Kings 20:6). Also, God can replace or provide a substitute for you as He did for Abraham (Gen. 22:13).

However, one thing God cannot do is to abolish sacrifice. All through the Bible, there's no single instance where God abolished sacrifice or promised to do so. Time can be taken out of the equation. Seed can be substituted. Sacrifice is not only absolute but expedient. Now you can ask and receive the same moment. That's a great news!

Wisdom, not age. Elihu was quick to remind Job and his three friends that wisdom is not of age. Listen to him. "I said, Days should speak, and multitude of years should teach wisdom. But there is a spirit in man: and the inspiration of the Almighty giveth them understanding. Great men are not always wise: neither do the aged understand judgment" (Job 32:7–9). Elihu's heart was filled with words and his lips "utter knowledge clearly" even as he said that, "The spirit of the God hath made me, and breath of the Almighty hath given me life" (Job 33:3–4).

God of utterance. Most importantly, Elihu told his audience that God speaks. Hear him. "For God speaketh once, yea twice, yet man perceiveth it not. In a dream, in a vision of the night, when deep sleep falleth upon men, in slumberings upon the bed; Then he openeth the ears of men, and sealeth their instruction, That he may withdraw man from his purpose, and hide pride from man" (Job 33:14–17).

Essentially, Elihu said that the problem was not with God. He always speak to us. The problem is always with man, who often rejects knowledge and in the process miss the opportunity of a shared experience in Christ. Job had no answers to the younger man divine exposition. It was useless for Job to continue to speak because he had no knowledge about what he was saying. "Therefore doth Job open his mouth in vain; he multiplieth word without knowledge" (Job 35:16).

When the *Lord* stepped into the scene, it was out of the whirlwind. You may ask which whirlwind? The same storm that was rocking Job. Psalms 50:3–4 says, "Our God shall come, and shall not keep silence: a fire shall devour before him, and it shall be very tempestuous round about him. He shall call to the heavens from above, and to the earth, that he may judge his people." Jesus rode the storm. God is always in your storm. He will wait to ensure that your soul is preserved. Afterall He promised never to leave you nor forsake you. Therefore whenever your storm rages, remember that God is always there. The scripture in Job 38:1–2 says, "Then the LORD answered Job out of the whirlwind, and said, Who is this that darkeneth counsel by words without knowledge?" Again, "Then answered the LORD unto Job out of the whirlwind, and said" (Job 40:6). He calls heaven and earth as witnesses to see Him judge His people.

Twice the Lord answered Job out of the whirlwind. You must not make the mistake of thinking that you have a distant God especially when you are in your season of storm. Jesus was asleep when the storm raged. When His disciples awoke Him, He arose and rebuked the storm. The wind ceased and there was a great calm (Mark 4:37).

It was obvious that Job suffered from lack of knowledge. He didn't know God intimately. Wisdom is the application of knowledge hence without knowledge, wisdom was far from Job. If wisdom was far, understanding was beyond reach. Understanding is a product of intimacy with God.

GRACE IN HIS BOSOM

Job was in the habit of sanctifying his children (Job 1:5). The act of sanctification by Job clearly points to a lack of knowledge. Sanctification belongs to God. It is the prerogative of the priesthood. The Bible neither told us if Job was of the tribe of Levites nor was he consecrated as a priest. Essentially, sanctification was the ritual that gave credence to his ignorance. His problem began after his priestly actions. That disruptive account must not be considered a coincidence. God is pointing us to a serious spiritual egregious infraction with severe consequences.

Finally, Job acknowledged his ignorance and surrendered completely to the Lord. Listen to him.

> Who is he that hideth counsel without knowledge? therefore have I uttered that I understood not; things too wonderful for me, which I knew not. Hear, I beseech thee, and I will speak: I will demand of thee, and declare thou unto me. I have heard of thee by the hearing of the ear: but now mine eye seeth thee. Wherefore I abhor myself and repent in dust and ashes. (Job 42:3–6)

Job's ordeal effectively ended when God appeared to him, and he knew Him personally. That's exactly what God desires of us-that we may know Him in a personal relationship. Job saw God as The Almighty. When God appears to you, it's a divine acknowledgment of your act of obedience and trust. He appeared to Abraham in Genesis 12. First,

God spoke. When Abraham obeyed, then He appeared the next time.

Happily, the Lord turned his captivity around and blessed him "twice as much as he had before" (Job 42:10). God showed up as a Father—ever forgiving, ever loving, and forever blessing.

Lessons of Job. The lessons of Job is sum up in Proverbs 3:5–7 as follows. (1) Trust in the Lord with all your heart. (2) In all your ways acknowledge Him. (2) Do not be wise in your own understanding. Colossians 1:9 says, "For this cause we also, since the day we heard it, do not cease to pray for you, and to desire that ye might be filled with the knowledge of his will in all wisdom and spiritual under-standing." It is the desire of God that you might be filled with the knowledge of His will in all wisdom and spiritual understanding. Knowledge is the key to receiving from God. It is dangerous to set your own rules in your relationship with God. It is imperative to know and follow His way. Job demonstrated so much faith but his faith was not mixed with knowledge.

He aptly portrayed the words of Hebrews 4:2, which states that the word didn't profit them because it was not mixed with faith. In similar manner, faith cannot prevail if your knowledge base is shallow. Faith thrives on believe and believe spring from knowledge. God wants you to know Him; that you may be strong and do exploits (Dan. 11:32). Job didn't know his God, hence he wasn't strong. On three occasions, God charged Joshua to "be strong and courageous." In the Book of Joshua 1:8; Joshua pointed us to where he derived his strength. "This book of the law shall not depart out of thy mouth; but thou shalt meditate therein day and night, that thou mayest observe to do according to all that is written therein: for then thou shalt make thy way prosperous, and then thou shalt have good success."

Water flow out of the temple. The water of Ezekiel 47 flows out of the temple. "Afterward he brought me again unto the door of the house; and, behold, waters issued out from under the threshold of the house eastward: for the forefront of the house stood toward the east, and the waters came down from under from the right side of the house, at the south side of the altar." The house under reference is the house of the Lord. It is the temple. Notice the presence of the altar. Of greater significance is the threshold. The threshold represents the Holy of Holies. The Holy of Holies is the most sacred portion of the temple only accessible to the chief priests. I perceive that it was at the Holy of Holies where Zacharias had an encounter with Angel Gabriel prior to the conception of his destiny son, John. "And the people waited for Zacharias, and marvelled that he tarried so long in the temple. And when he came out, he could not speak unto them: and they perceived that he had seen a vision in the temple: for he beckoned unto them, and remained speechless" (Luke 1:21–22). The people couldn't get into the sacred spot. They simply waited in the outer court even as Zacharias the chief priest tarried. The water was coming from under the Holy of Holies. That's the minting place of the Word of God. The word was poured out in liquid form so that you could be cleansed and washed in it.

Jesus the Word

Jesus says, "The thief cometh not, but for to steal, and to kill, and to destroy: I am come that they might have life, and that they might have it more abundantly" (John 10:10). Jesus is The Word. John 1:1–2 says, "In the beginning was the Word, and the Word was with God, and the Word was God. The same was in the beginning with God." The beginning predates Genesis 1. It began at the threshold of the temple. The last place the devil took Jesus was atop the temple. In Matthew 4:5, the Bible recorded, "Then the devil taketh him up into the holy city, and setteth him on a pinnacle of the temple." Luke 4:9 puts it this way, "And he brought him to Jerusalem, and set him on a pinnacle of the temple, and said unto him, If thou be the Son of God, cast thyself down from hence."

The tempter took Jesus back to the beginning-where it all started. The enemy will always remind you of your past. Glory to God that the unemployed cherub was never part of the beginning hence the devil can never get into your beginning. He can only remind you of the circumstances and situations—those peripheral issues surrounding your past. The tempter brought Jesus to Jerusalem only to set Him on the pinnacle of the temple. The enemy is disqualified from the threshold of the temple where it all began because light and darkness can't cohabit. The devil represents darkness and darkness can't understand light. "And the light shineth in darkness and darkness comprehended it not" (John 1:3).

Truth is, the devil doesn't really know you. He was never there in the beginning, hence the picture of your past that he flaunts so often is nothing but a panoramic view. It is what lawyers call circumstantial evidence. The pinnacle presents a panoramic view as it is with a peripheral perspective. Joyfully, you are fearfully and wonderfully made to reflect the glory of God. When next the devil shows up, declare to him that greater is He that is in you than he (the enemy) that is in the world. "Ye are of God, little children, and have overcome them: because greater is he that is in you, than he that is in the world" (1 John 4:4). Even darkness in all demonic densities can never comprehend you because you were called out of darkness into His marvelous light. "But ye are a chosen generation, a royal priesthood, an holy nation, a peculiar people; that ye should shew forth the praises of him who hath called you out of darkness into his marvellous light" (1 Peter 2:9).

Threshold of the Word. The word springs from under the threshold. The river of Ezekiel 37 took its rise from the *Source.* During His earthly ministry, Jesus our High Priest was always in the temple. That was His office address and the headquarters of His Father's business. After three days of searching for Jesus, His earthly parents found Him exactly where they left Him—the temple. "And he said unto them, How is it that ye sought me? wist ye not that I must be about my Father's business?" (Luke 2:49). The temple is where the business of the Lord is conducted. That's why you must go to church to acquaint yourself of our Father's business. If you desire Kingdom knowledge, you must go to church. The church is the Springfield of knowledge. Knowledge issues out from under the threshold of the temple. Every river has its source.

It was the custom of Jesus to return to the temple where it all began. "And he taught in their synagogues, being glorified of all. And he came to Nazareth, where he had been brought up: and, as his custom was, he went into the synagogue on the sabbath day, and stood up for to read" (Luke 4:15–16). It was the custom of Jesus to touch base with the beginning. Every river has its source. That source represents the beginning. Rivers take their rise from tiny springs. The water flows outward, defines a course unto the sea. God says, "The earth shall be full of the knowledge of the LORD as the waters cover the sea" (Isa. 11:9). You are created to flow with the waters that cover the sea.

You are the temple. The knowledge of God flows from the temple. You are the temple of God. His Spirit lives in you. "Know ye not that ye are the temple of God, and that the Spirit of God dwelleth in you?" (1 Cor. 3:16). The Spirit of the Lord God dwells in your heart for that is the threshold of the temple. The Kingdom of God is within you. It is like a garden planted in your heart. Conscious of that "In the last day, that great day of the feast, Jesus stood and cried, saying, If any man thirst, let him come unto me, and drink. He that believeth on me, as the scripture hath said, out of his belly shall flow rivers of living water" (John 7:37–38).

God desires that your knowledge of Him will continually flow out of your innermost being. It is not flowing from you. They are not your word. They are flowing out of you. The scripture says, the "waters issued from under the threshold of the house…" They were not the words of the priest hence they didn't emanate from your pastor. It is the design of God that you become a moving threshold for the outpouring of His knowledge and the Jesus experience which is wrapped in love.

God as a Surveyor

Ezekiel 47:3–5 is the account of "man that had the line in his hand." That scripture is a portrayal of a surveyor or engineer with a measuring tape. He took measurements at regular intervals of a thousand cubits. A thousand cubits is equivalent to 560 yards. He repeated the routine four times. The significance of that exercise is that your relationship with God is quantifiable. You can measure it. Definitely, God factors it into scale. What the man had in his hand was a scale. The critical question: why must God bring to ratio your knowledge of His Kingdom or even your relationship with Him?

In Jeremiah 29:11, the scripture says, "For I know the thoughts that I think toward you, saith the LORD, thoughts of peace, and not of evil, to give you an expected end." The New American Standard Bible (NASB) puts it this way. "For I know the plans that I have for you, declares the LORD, plans for welfare and not for calamity to give you a future and a hope." Truth is, engineers and people in the physical sciences can hardly go to work without a scale. Scale is described as the ratio of the distance on maps or plan to that on the ground. Scale is important for the objective assessment of their assignment. When God spoke about plans in Jeremiah 29:11, He meant something concrete and cemented. A plan is concrete. It is specific and measurable. Most importantly, a plan is achievable because it is factored into scale. There's no plan without a scale.

The opposite of a plan is a sketch. A sketch is very general hence it is speculative and not measurable. The scale accounts for the difference between a plan and a sketch. Oftentimes, you learn of verbiage such as sketch-plan. Those two words can never stand for the same stuff. Man can't produce a hybrid of sketch and plan. It is either a sketch or a plan. With God, there are no probabilities. God is a God of absolute certainty. His words are yea and amen. "Every good gift and every perfect gift is from above, and cometh down from the Father of lights, with whom is no variableness, neither shadow of turning" (James 1:17).

God is unchangeable and doesn't cause darkness. He remains the same yesterday, today and forever. God works with both sketch and plan. The covenant moves of destiny usually starts with a sketch and progress to the plan.

Sketch to plan. The land surveyor developed a principle known as "working from whole to part." It is very simple. Point a parcel of land to the surveyor, his first assignment would be to go round the perimeter. The perimeter is the external boundary of the property which is akin to the whole. Thereafter, the surveyor begins to "cut" the parcel of land into smaller pieces of varying triangles which represent the parts. In that manner, he could work faster, minimize errors, and make calculations easier. In a nutshell, the surveyor worked from whole to part.

GRACE IN HIS BOSOM

God works from whole to part because He knows the end from the beginning. "I am Alpha and Omega, the beginning and the end, the first and the last" (Rev. 22:13).

Sketch for Abraham. In Genesis 12, the Bible recorded an account of the evolving relationship between God and Abram. The Lord spoke to Abram the first time and Abram departed.

> Now the LORD had said unto Abram, Get thee out of thy country, and from thy kindred, and from thy father's house, unto a land that I will shew thee: And I will make of thee a great nation, and I will bless thee, and make thy name great; and thou shalt be a blessing: And I will bless them that bless thee, and curse him that curseth thee: and in thee shall all families of the earth be blessed. So Abram departed, as the LORD had spoken unto him; and Lot went with him: and Abram was seventy and five years old when he departed out of Haran. (Gen. 12:1–4)

When Abram obeyed God and took a step of faith, something dramatic and tangible happened in verse 7. The Lord appeared unto Abram. "And the LORD appeared unto Abram, and said, Unto thy seed will I give this land: and there builded he an altar unto the LORD, who appeared unto him" (Gen. 12:7). Notice that the first time, the LORD only said. The second time the LORD appeared.

The first instruction was very general. That was the sketch. The second as recorded in verse 7, was direct and specific. It was specific because the LORD said, "I will give this land." Nothing becomes dynamic until it becomes specific. What moved Abraham's destiny from sketch to plan was simply his obedience. And because Abram obeyed, the LORD appeared. Whenever the LORD appears, that's when your journey of intimacy begins. Every visitation culminates in distinction. However, that instruction was not yet a plan until Abram did something.

Scale of worship. If you wanted to build a house, your foremost move would be to tell the architect what you want. In designing the plan, the architect will introduce a scale. That was the scenario for Abram (Gen. 12:1–7). The first time God spoke to Abram, he made a sketch. God appeared and spoke for the second time, Abram introduced a scale. Genesis 12:7 (in part) says, "And there builded he an altar unto the LORD who appeared unto him."

Place of altar

The altar is your place of assessment. It is the connection to the One you worship. The altar is designed to keep you in focus and to alert you whenever you derail from the trajectory of your glorious destiny. Consequently, the altar constitutes the reference point. It is apex of your commitment. A return to the altar is critical to the assessment of your Kingdom journey. When Abram left the place of his altar, he couldn't stop moving (Gen. 12 and 13). Put differently, Abram had no peace. With all his riches, peace

GRACE IN HIS BOSOM

eluded him because he abandoned the reference point, yea the scale. Abram abandoned the scale and the building of his life couldn't proceed according to the plan of God. It developed structural defects which manifested in anxiety. Notwithstanding, Abram was rich because the anointing was on him and not on the plan. If you jettison the plan of God for your life, you may have riches but not peace. Moving from place to place is a serious symptom of anxiety.

> And Abram went up out of Egypt, he, and his wife, and all that he had, and Lot with him, into the south. And Abram was very rich in cattle, in silver, and in gold. And he went on his journeys from the south even to Beth-el, unto the place where his tent had been at the beginning, between Beth-el and Hai; Unto the place of the altar, which he had made there at the first: and there Abram called on the name of the LORD. (Gen. 13:1–4)

The scripture enjoined us to be anxious for nothing. "Be careful for nothing; but in every thing by prayer and supplication with thanksgiving let your requests be made known unto God. And the peace of God, which passeth all understanding, shall keep your hearts and minds through Christ Jesus" (Phil. 4:6–7).

Absence of anxiety is the enthronement of peace. Abram could not worship God until he returned to his place of altar. The altar is not only where you worship God, it is the compass and barometer of your life. It points to the direction and at the same time deflate the pressure associated with your journey irrespective of the altitudes you attained in riches and wealth.

Peace is never ushered on the platform of the cares of the world. Peace is given when you remain connected to the Prince of Peace. In all of Abram's sojourn, worship was absent until he returned to the place where he built an altar. The scripture says, "There he worshiped the LORD." Truth is, care of this world can't allow you to worship the LORD.

Haven noted that distraction, Jesus asked us to as a matter of priorities, seek the Kingdom of God and its righteousness. "But seek ye first the kingdom of God, and his righteousness; and all these things shall be added unto you" (Matt. 6:33). Seeking the Kingdom first guarantees peace. "For thus saith the LORD unto the house of Israel, Seek ye me, and ye shall live" (Amos 5:4).

Of altar and seed. The altar that receives your seed shall speak for you. At the height of Jacob's crisis of mutual distrust with uncle Laban, the Angel who spoke to Jacob in a dream announced its constituency in this manner: "I am the God of Beth-el, where thou anointedst the pillar, and where thou vowedst a vow unto me: now arise, get thee out from this land, and return unto the land of thy kindred" (Gen. 31:13). Alas! the God of Jacob's altar where he sowed the seed by vow, came to his rescue. When Laban pursued Jacob and overtook him, the God of his altar came to Laban in a dream. "And God came to Laban the Syrian in a dream by night, and said unto him, Take heed that thou speak not to Jacob either good or bad" (Gen. 31:24). At a critical moment in Jacob's life, the God of his altar intervened. The God of your altar will always speak to and for you.

Power to preach

The power was to be operational after the burial and resurrection of Jesus. Jesus had in Matthew 26:12 said,

> "For in that she had poured this ointment on my body, she did it for my burial." The great commission which put the power in effect, was issued after Jesus rose from the dead. And Jesus came and spake unto them, saying, "All power is given unto me in heaven and in earth. Go ye therefore, and teach all nations, baptizing them in the name of the Father, and of the Son, and of the Holy Ghost: Teaching them to observe all things whatsoever I have commanded you: and, lo, I am with you alway, even unto the end of the world. Amen." (Matt. 28:18–20)

Learn to receive. The major challenge of man is in the area of receiving spiritual things. In his awesomeness, God aforetime released all promises concerning you. No doubt, man, have demonstrated, dismal track record of receiving the things of God. Our major phrase remains: God give me this or that. It is difficult to understand how God can give you all over again, the things which He had afore-time released to you. Time is now for you to learn how to receive from God. Ask the Holy Spirit for help. "He will keep the feet of his saints, and the wicked shall be silent in darkness; for by strength shall no man prevail" (1 Sam. 2:9).

Enter the Holy Ghost

To help man out of his predicament, Jesus, in Acts 1:8 says, "But ye shall receive power, after that the Holy Ghost is come upon you: and ye shall be witnesses unto me both in Jerusalem, and in all Judaea, and in Samaria, and unto the uttermost part of the earth." The Holy Ghost came to help man receive the power that was released. The very power of the knowledge of God that started when the woman broke the alabaster box and poured it on the head of Jesus, could only be received with the help of the Holy Ghost. When the woman anointed Jesus with the ointment, the aroma filled the house but not the people. The sweet savor followed Mary home because she wiped the feet of Jesus with her hair but it never filled her. I perceive that because of the strong aromatic fragrance, it probably followed everyone present home. Nevertheless, it didn't fill the Apostle until the advent of the Holy Ghost on the day of Pentecost.

> And when the day of Pentecost was fully come, they were all with one accord in one place. And suddenly there came a sound from heaven as of a rushing mighty

> wind, and it filled all the house where they were sitting. And there appeared unto them cloven tongues like as of fire, and it sat upon each of them. And they were all filled with the Holy Ghost, and began to speak with other tongues, as the Spirit gave them utterance. (Acts 2:4)

In John 12:3, "The house was filled with the odour of the ointment." Also, when the Holy Ghost came as a rushing mighty wind, "it filled all the house where they were sitting." It follows that both the knowledge and the power filled the house but not the people. Until the Holy Ghost did something to sheathe the flesh, the apostles could not be filled. The Holy Ghost baptized them with fire. In the first instance, the woman poured the ointment on the head of Jesus to trigger the ventilation of the aroma of knowledge whereas the Holy Ghost in the second instance, baptized them with fire that sat upon their heads. The "cloven tongues like as a fire" were to burn off their flesh. The flesh is symbolic of the way of thinking that is contrary to the word and knowledge of God. As soon as that was done, "they were all filled with the Holy Ghost and began to speak with other tongues, as the Spirit gave them utterance." Knowledge and power coalesced.

The significance of what the woman did with the ointment could never be fully comprehended. The Spirit that gave the apostles utterance, was also present at the meeting where Mary anointed Jesus. The wind that ventilated the house on that fateful day was the same wind that blew where it chose and no one could tell where it comes or goes (John 3:8). That wind made sure that fragrance filled the house. If the woman had decided to drop the ointment on her palm and rub it on His head; I perceive that it would have had a limited impact. But she poured it. What gets in the head, get to the feet. When she broke and poured it out, in an act of righteous violence, the wind ventilated the house and the aroma was in all directions. The impact was unrestricted and unlimited.

In similar fashion, when the apostles were filled with the Holy Ghost, they began to speak with other tongues because when the aroma of the knowledge of God went out, it had unrestricted impact. Your utterance travels with the wind. Wherever the wind can penetrate, such is the utterance that the Spirit has given to you. It was neither restricted to the Jews nor the Greek, the English, the Roman and Albanians. Anywhere that the wind could reach, the same have the Holy Ghost given you utterance.

Mary and Jesus ministry

Glory to God for the life of our mothers. Through the womb of Mary, God gave to the world the precious gift of His beloved Son Jesus Christ. Also, mother Mary mid-wife the miraculous ministry of Jesus Christ. Prior to the miracle at the wedding in Cana of Galilee, Jesus ministry was basically a teaching one. Again, another Mary with the gift of her expensive fragrance made sure that the aroma of the knowledge of God was not restricted to the classroom

GRACE IN HIS BOSOM

teaching of Jesus Christ. It was not a coincidence that both women were known as Mary. The knowledge of God is sweet like a smelling fragrance. Strive to attain the highest standard so that when the enemy comes like a flood, the Spirit of the Lord will locate an appreciable standard in you to mitigate the challenges.

Religious, yet lost. Someone could be religious yet lost. Nicodemus was such a man. Ditto Job. When Nicodemus approached Jesus in the wee hours of the morning, sought to resolve a nudging question; he was completely a lost man. Make no mistake a about that, Nicodemus was a Pharisee and a ruler. Such positions are never reserved for the unlearned and uncivilized of the society. His position was considered the amalgamation of religious and royal interests. The Pharisees were held in high esteem unto this day.

> There was a man of the Pharisees, named Nicodemus, a ruler of the Jews: The same came to Jesus by night, and said unto him, Rabbi, we know that thou art a teacher come from God: for no man can do these miracles that thou doest, except God be with him. Jesus answered and said unto him, Verily, verily, I say unto thee, Except a man be born again, he cannot see the kingdom of God. Nicodemus saith unto him, How can a man be born when he is old? can he enter the second time into his mother's womb, and be born? Jesus

answered, Verily, verily, I say unto thee, Except a man be born of water and of the Spirit, he cannot enter into the kingdom of God. That which is born of the flesh is flesh; and that which is born of the Spirit is spirit. Marvel not that I said unto thee, Ye must be born again. The wind bloweth where it listeth, and thou hearest the sound thereof, but canst not tell whence it cometh, and whither it goeth: so is every one that is born of the Spirit. Nicodemus answered and said unto him, How can these things be? Jesus answered and said unto him, Art thou a master of Israel, and knowest not these things? Verily, verily, I say unto thee, We speak that we do know, and testify that we have seen; and ye receive not our witness. If I have told you earthly things, and ye believe not, how shall ye believe, if I tell you of heavenly things? And no man hath ascended up to heaven, but he that came down from heaven, even the Son of man which is in heaven. And as Moses lifted up the serpent in the wilderness, even so must the Son of man be lifted up: That whosoever believeth in him should not perish, but have eternal life. For God so loved the world, that he gave his only begotten Son, that whosoever believeth in him should not perish, but have everlasting life. For God sent not his Son into the world to condemn the world; but that the world through him might be saved. He that believeth on him is not condemned: but he that believeth not is condemned already, because he hath not believed in the name of the only begotten Son of God. And this is the condemnation, that light is come into the world, and men loved darkness rather than light, because their deeds were evil. For every one that doeth evil hateth the light, neither cometh to the light, lest his deeds should be reproved. But he that doeth truth cometh to the light, that his deeds may be made manifest, that they are wrought in God. (John 3:1–21)

Consider the amount of light that shone from a single meeting of a pious and religious ruler with Jesus. If not for that meeting, mankind would have been lost completely. It seems to me that Job was the first Nicodemus but because he never had a meeting with God, he was lost until God intervened. Unlike David, Job worshipped a God he didn't know. He feared a God he didn't know either. These claims may appear controversial but are true. Throughout scriptures, David knew the God that he worshipped. He was in regular fellowship with God. On the other hand, there was no account where Job reasoned together with God. God had a meeting with everyone including Satan but never with job until He thundered like a whirlwind in chapter 38 to reprimand him.

God prescribes the way He should be worshipped—for them that worship God must do so in spirit and in truth. It follows that you cannot worship Him until you know the truth. The truth you know will set you free. It is the spirit of liberty that provokes acceptable worship. For in His presence is the fullness of joy and at His right hand are pleasures forever. It is impossible to worship God and not experience inner peace and joy. "And they worshipped him and returned to Jerusalem with great joy" (Luke 24:25).

Did Job break a hedge?

Permit me once again to return to our man Job. Somehow he has become a case study for us in this matter. It is difficult to stop marvelling how easy it was for Satan to obtain permission to punish Job. God gave an express permission for Satan to punish a man He described as "upright and just." If that doesn't startle you, then nothing would. Nonetheless, a deeper look at the entire story of Job would reveal to you that God cannot contradict Himself. "If we believe not, yet he abideth faithful: he cannot deny himself" (2 Tim. 2:13).

In Ecclesiastes, the scripture pointed out that "He that diggeth a pit shall fall into it; and whoso breaketh an hedge, a serpent shall bite him" (Eccles. 10:8). Notice that the problem of Job began immediately after what he did in Job 1:5. The entire story took a sudden turn after what Job did. That's very significant. In a nutshell, Job took upon

GRACE IN HIS BOSOM

himself a role that transcends that of a father. Throughout Bible history, none of the patriarchs sanctified their children. Abraham blessed Isaac. Isaac blessed Jacob and Esau. Jacob blessed his children. None of the patriarchs of our faith, at any instance, purified their children. Even Isaac, the child of promise, was never purified by Abraham.

However, that was not the case with Job as he was in the habit of purifying his sons and daughters.

> And his sons went and feasted in their houses, every one his day; and sent and called for their three sisters to eat and to drink with them. And it was so, when the days of their feasting were gone about, that Job sent and sanctified them, and rose up early in the morning, and offered burnt offerings according to the number of them all: for Job said, It may be that my sons have sinned, and cursed God in their hearts. Thus did Job continually. (Job 1:4–5)

Out of ignorance, sanctification became a pleasant ritual for Job. Truth is, sanctification belongs to God. It is the authority of the priesthood. Sanctification usually follows a divine instruction and it is the prerogative of the priesthood. Jesus is our High Priest. Job was a good man for God declared so. Notwithstanding, he failed to add knowledge to his goodness. Second Peter 1:5 put it succinctly: "And besides this, giving all diligence, add to your faith virtue and to virtue knowledge." Every act of goodness must have a knowledge domain. Job worshipped God faithfully but it's an irony that he didn't know the God that he worshipped. He was a good man, careful not to do anything wrong but out of ignorance, he did one stupid thing that is classified as mutiny in Kingdom constitution. God was aware that Job's worship was to Him but God would not study His word for Job (Job 1:8).

God has poured His word out to you like He did for every other Job out there. To study the Word of God is a nontransferable responsibility of man. God cannot do that for you or to anyone else. Regrettably, Job failed to recognize that truth and that was his failure.

Don't get me wrong. You can purify yourself but you can't perform that function on others, if you are not chosen, irrespective of your relationship with them. At best, what spiritual gift you can give to your children is to pray for them and bless them. With the best of intentions, Job did the wrong thing which became his stronghold. Satan knows the scripture for he is a fallen angel. Oftentimes, Satan goes to church to obtain express permission to punish the Jobs of this world, who are breaking God's law out of ignorance. God doesn't blink over anything that has to do with priesthood. If in doubt, read the account of the rebellion of Korah, Dathan and Abiram against Aaron and Moses in Numbers 16:1–35.

Specifically in verse 10, Moses accused them of trying to capture the priesthood. Listen to him. "And he hath brought thee near to him, and all thy brethren the sons of Levi with thee: and seek ye the priesthood also?" (Num.

16:10). The wrath of God fell on Dathan and Abiram and their families. The ground under them split open and swallowed them. To undertake a spiritual function you are not called for is tantamount to suicide. God reserved the priesthood for Himself hence Jesus is our High Priest, who has the power to restore us to the original state of Adam. Those words of Moses apply even to the Korah's of today. All you pastors, deacons, deaconess, ushers, sanctuary keepers, hospitality workers, choir, protocol, welfare, men, and women groups, etc.—all whom God had brought closer to Himself, "to do the service of the tabernacle of the LORD, and to stand before the congregation to minister unto them." Please leave the priesthood alone. It is futile to envy the priesthood or murmur against it. Abraham, the father of faith, was not called to priesthood and he never assumed so.

Priesthood is for the chosen

Every high priest is chosen from his fellowmen and appointed to serve God on their behalf to offer sacrifices and offerings for sins. The high priest is supposed to be a broken vessel. In brokenness, he is weak in many ways. That way, he should be able to be gentle with those who are ignorant and make mistakes. Since weakness is all-over him, he must offer sacrifices not only for the sins of the people but also for his own sins. No one chooses for himself the honor of being a high priest. It is only by God's call that a man is made a high priest, just as the case of Aaron.

Christ did not take upon himself the honor of being a high priest. Pointedly, God said to Him, "You are my Son; today I have become your Father." Again, He said, "You will be a priest forever, in the priestly order of Melchizedek."

Priestly sacred duties. There are two sacred duties that priests perform. They sanctify and they receive tithe. Abraham recognized that when he gave his tithe to Melchizedek-a king who ascended the priesthood. Genesis 14:18 says, "And Melchizedek king of Salem brought forth bread and wine: and he was the priest of the most high God." In Ezekiel 18:4 God says, "Behold, all souls are mine; as the soul of the father, so also the soul of the son is mine: the soul that sinneth, it shall die." Only God can sanctify. Him alone can purify. It is part of the responsibility of the priest. Even the Levites whom God set aside to serve Him cannot assume such sacred responsibility. Hear Moses.

> And Moses said unto Korah, Hear, I pray you, ye sons of Levi: Seemeth it but a small thing unto you, that the God of Israel hath separated you from the congregation of Israel, to bring you near to himself to do the service of the tabernacle of the LORD, and to stand before the congregation to minister unto them? And he hath brought thee near to him, and all thy brethren the sons of Levi with thee: and seek ye the priesthood also? (Num. 16:8–10)

From the words of Moses, being a Levi is not synonymous with priesthood.

Sanctification is a sacred ritual done for the atonement of sin. It is different from burnt offerings. The Bible is littered with records of burnt offerings by individuals and groups. Anyone in relationship with God can offer burnt offerings to God. Noah was the first to do so and the Lord smelled a sweet savor.

> And Noah builded an altar unto the LORD; and took of every clean beast, and of every clean fowl, and offered burnt offerings on the altar. And the LORD smelled a sweet savour; and the LORD said in his heart, I will not again curse the ground any more for man's sake; for the imagination of man's heart is evil from his youth; neither will I again smite any more every thing living, as I have done. (Gen. 8:20–21)

Abraham offered Isaac for a burnt offerings but God substituted his seed with a ram (Gen. 22:12–13). Ditto Moses and so on. God is often pleased with burnt offerings. It is important to note that all those that offered burnt offerings to God were in conversation with Him. They established some measure of intimacy with God. That was not the case with Job. There was no recorded conversation between God and Job until God spoke out of the whirlwind. Sanctification is of a higher order and office because it has to do with purification and cleansing. It is not of the purification of the flesh but of the soul.

The soul of man belongs to God. Never did God give man authority over his own soul. "Behold, all souls are mine; and the soul of the father, so..." It is expedient that we learn from the experience of Job. Essentially, there are many Jobs around us since ignorance still rules the air. Specifically, Job did two things before the crisis. (1) He sanctified his children. (2) He offered burnt offerings. The two activities were not done at the same time. He sanctified them before he rose early in the morning and offered burnt offerings according to the number of them all. The two are not the same and do not serve the same purpose.

No place for assumption

Again, Job assumed that it may be that his sons have sinned and cursed God in their hearts (Job 1:5). Notwithstanding that God called Job "my servant" and described him as "perfect and upright" it is obvious, from the foregoing that Job had no personal relationship with God. If he did, the Spirit of the Lord would have revealed things to him. God is not a God of probability. There's no room for assumption when you are in a relationship with God. His law and principles are well lettered in the Bible. God is a God of absolute certainty.

Everything that happened to Job points to ignorance. "My people are destroyed for lack of knowledge: because thou hast rejected knowledge, I will also reject thee, that thou shalt be no priest to me: seeing thou hast forgotten the law of thy God, I will also forget thy children" (Hos. 4:6). Notice the link between knowledge and priesthood in the scripture above. Without knowledge, priesthood is never to be contemplated.

God is a God of mercy, loving kindness, and compassion. Jesus never ignored the cry for mercy. "It is the LORD'S mercies that we are not consumed, because his compassions fail not. They are new every morning: great is thou faithfulness" (Lam. 3:22–23).

In Hebrews 5, it is obvious that the LORD choses people to be ordained into priesthood.

> For every high priest taken from among men is ordained for men in things pertaining to God, that he may offer both gifts and sacrifices for sins: Who can have compassion on the ignorant, and on them that are out of the way; for that he himself also is compassed with infirmity. And by reason hereof he ought, as for the people, so also for himself, to offer for sins. And no man taketh this honour unto himself, but he that is called of God, as was Aaron. So also Christ glorified not himself to be made an high priest; but he that said unto him, Thou art my Son, to day have I begotten thee. As he saith also in another place, Thou art a priest for ever after the order of Melchisedec. (Heb. 5:1–6)

The problem that buffeted Job, which was clearly captured in what he did continually in Job 1:5, have a veiled reference in the above scripture. After going through the scripture above and you are still in doubt about what triggered the problem of Job; you might as well consider yourself in league with him. Whoah! The revelations are mind blowing. Job was religious but ignorant. The same God that called him a perfect and upright man before Satan, also called him ignorant to his face. "Who are you to question my wisdom with your ignorant, empty words?" (Job 38:2 Good News Bible). You can be a kind hearted and generous man but as the saying goes, "ignorance is no excuse."

A relationship with God that is not based upon a robust Kingdom knowledge derived from His word is warped and capable of turning you into an ignorant person. It doesn't matter how educated or qualified you are. God is the Grand Qualifier and He qualifies you on the basis of the knowledge of His words. The integrity of God's word will never be sacrificed. They are One and The Same. Generally, the Book of Job is full of mysteries. They are mysteries dedicated to human sufferings. May the Lord open your eyes.

Hear what God said about the people of Hosea 4:6, a destination where the Jobs of this world live. "My people are destroyed for lack of knowledge: because thou hast rejected knowledge, I will also reject thee, that thou shalt be no priest to me: seeing thou hast forgotten the law of thy God, I will also forget thy children." Pay attention and you will discover the man Job in that scripture. No knowledge, no priesthood. You can't assume the role of a priest not even over your family, if you are not called to that office. Job's life was mired in contradictions. A "perfect and upright man" who feared God and avoided evil. He was roundly religious but ignorant. Out of ignorance and for the love of children, he perfected a sacred priestly tradition, hence he broke an hedge and a serpent inflicted him terribly. He lost everything including the children he loved so much. At the end, he was cleansed, purified, and sanctified by the High Priest. Job was restored by "The repairer of the breach, The restorer of the paths to dwell in" (Isa. 58:12) who multiplied by two whatsoever Job lost. How wonderful the way of God!

One thing you can't do. It is often the pleasure of every father to enthuse, "I can do anything for my children." There are a number of things you can't do for your children especially when it comes to spiritual matters. Father is automatic as soon as you have a child. As a father, you can give offerings, sow seeds and sacrifice on behalf of your children but never assume priesthood over your children. It runs contrary to the Word of God. God gave you a mouth and a wisdom to which no adversary can withstand or gainsay. Therefore, open your mouth wide, pray, and bless your children. Don't attempt to purify or sanctify them in any form; for you are not called to that sacred office. Even if you are of the tribe of the Levites, you still have to be called to priesthood. "But ye shall be named the Priests of the LORD: men shall call you the Ministers of our God: ye shall eat the riches of the Gentiles, and in their glory shall ye boast yourselves" (Isa. 61:6). Until you are named, don't assume any priestly role or responsibility. God in exercise of His divine sovereignty and prerogative chose vessels and channels through whom to administer His divine plans. There's no suggestion in the scripture that God has renounced His right to do so.

What to do when you hurt

Throughout Job's agonizing ordeal, you could see hurt written all over him. Anytime you hurt, it is better to look inward. When you do, you will notice that whatever situation you are going through provides a teachable experience, either to refine or humble you.

The people of Psalm 66:12 put it this way. "Thou hast caused men to ride over our heads; we went through fire and through water: but thou broughtest us out into a wealthy place." The plan of God is to bring you to your place of abundance. It is the pleasure of Satan to inflict pain and hardship but don't like going through the same experience. That was where he missed wisdom and understanding. Satan is unemployed hence he roams "to and fro" the earth. Like an idle man, Satan is lazy and would not go through pain. He circumvents the rules to catch up on pleasures which translate to afflictions. Little wonder why the devil walks to and fro the earth, lurking around and waiting for someone who is at the point of his pleasure, to strike.

Consider the moment he chose to attack Job. It was party time, indeed a time of pleasure. Taking turns to celebrate was routine for the children (Job 1:13, 18–19). If Satan did it to Job and Samson, he could do it to anyone because he comes to steal, to kill and to destroy (John 10:10).

Jesus doesn't circumvent. He goes through the crucible of your life. The scripture in John 4:3 says, "And he must needs go through Samaria." It was absolutely necessary that Jesus went through Samaria. Certain things are allowed by God which He, in His sovereignty classify under must. Must is the language of a decree. Jesus could have avoided Samaria like the rest of the Jews but His divine trajectory on earth, was linked to a decree by the King of kings.

When Jesus passed through Samaria, He discovered a city and her people that were ready for the kingdom. Granted, God gave you the power of choice but often-times, life itself doesn't offer you many choices. Everyone has a Samaria "he must needs go through." It could be that uncomfortable circumstance that makes you to swallow your pride; a humbling experience. Every destiny is pro-grammed to get through water and fire experience. Potifa's wife was Joseph's Samaria. For David, it was Goliath. Moses confronted Pharaoh and Peter had to contend with Harod. Esther couldn't avoid Haman. Mordecai said to Esther, "And who knoweth whether thou hast come to the king-dom for such a time as this?" (Esther 4:14, in part).

The "must needs go through Samaria" event of your life is the very one that brings you to your point of "if I per-ish, I perish." Esther 4:16 says, "Go, gather together all the Jews that are present in Shushan, and fast ye for me, and neither eat nor drink three days, night or day: I also and my maidens will fast likewise; and so will I go in unto the king, which is not according to the law: and if I perish, I perish."

Such divinely ordained events don't happen twice in a lifetime as they become your processing chamber designed to bring you to your place of glory.

The only thing standing between you and your glorious destiny is fear. God programs such events to move you against your fear so that you can emerge at your place of abundance. The experience of going through water and fire is a necessary Kingdom requirement for arriving at your divine destination. Fear held Job hostage and caused him to do stupid things. He said, "For the thing which I greatly feared is come upon me, and that which I was afraid of is come unto me" (Job 3:25). God moved Job against his fear so that he may develop faith and manifest his destiny. For Job as it was for his forebears; it was an experience intended to humble and to prove in all facets of life. Deuteronomy 8:2 puts it succinctly. "And thou shalt remember all the way which the LORD thy God led thee these forty years in the wilderness, to humble thee, and to prove thee, to know what was in thine heart, whether thou wouldest keep his commandments, or no."

Job never sinned with his lips. He even reprimanded his wife for demanding that he curse God and die. "Then said his wife unto him, Dost thou still retain thine integrity? curse God, and die. But he said unto her, Thou speakest as one of the foolish women speaketh. What? shall we receive good at the hand of God, and shall we not receive evil? In all this did not Job sin with his lips" (Job 2:9–10). Before you shed those tears in agony, remember that so many faithfuls went through such experiences. In all of that, not one of them lost focus. No matter the experience you are going through, the one thing under contention is your Kingdom destiny. Let the kingdom remain your focus. If some plugs are malfunctioning in you, God will use that experience to clean them up, so that you can function at your full capacity in Christ.

Quest for intimacy

God is continually looking for a bedroom sort of intimate relationship with you. The following lines in Songs of Solomon portrays in graphic detail the sort of relationship God craves for. It will excite you in the same way that it will purge your spiritual lethargy.

> I sleep, but my heart waketh: it is the voice of my beloved that knocketh, saying, Open to me, my sister, my love, my dove, my undefiled: for my head is filled with dew, and my locks with the drops of the night. I have put off my coat; how shall I put it on? I have washed my feet; how shall I defile them? My beloved put in his hand by the hole of the door, and my bowels were moved for him. I rose up to open to my beloved; and my hands dropped with myrrh, and my fingers with sweet smelling myrrh, upon the handles of the lock. I opened to my beloved; but my beloved had withdrawn himself, and was gone: my soul failed when he spake:

I sought him, but I could not find him;
I called him, but he gave me no answer.
(Song of Solomon 5:2–6)

Jesus visited but His love, symbolically represented by the woman, who in turn portrayed our nonchalance and carelessness. Indeed, it was a story of a missed opportunity. The lady was hamstrung by the stronghold of cosmetics— those unnecessary and peripheral distractions. After God opened the door and left, the door handles were filled with myrrh. We know where myrrh came from. Myrrh was one of the first gifts presented to Jesus by the three wise men. The import of that story is that, God is continually into the kingdom business of visitations, as He seeks intimacy with His sons and daughters. If you miss the opportunity to receive Jesus, the result is frustration. There is no convenient time in the Kingdom and in every barrenness is a missed opportunity. Jesus will open the door but will never force you to receive Him. God left you with the power of choice.

When Jesus appeared to the disciples after His resurrection, the doors were locked (John 20:19 and 26). The environment of the divine is unrestricted. He is God Omnipresent. He is the wind that ventilates anywhere it chooses. Essentially, He chose to visit His friends behind closed doors, hence intimacy resonate with His presence.

Enter the overcomer. Job went through water and fire but emerged as an overcomer. "And the LORD turned the captivity of Job, when he prayed for his friends: also the LORD gave Job twice as much as he had before" (Job

GRACE IN HIS BOSOM

42:10). The word overcomer is of great value in heaven. To overcome is a testament of your successful resistance to the nefarious antics of the enemy. Job overcame. Daniel overcame as did the three Hebrew youths Shedrack, Meshach, and Abednego. As a traveler in the Kingdom journey, it is important that you identify the point, at which you step into your world of inheritance. God is emphatic about that. He made overcoming the condition for inheriting the world.

The last Book of the Bible emphasizes the importance of overcoming more than any other book. That occurrence was not accidental. It is the desire of God that after going through unpleasant situations, you must emerge as an overcomer. After paying the price, you receive the overcomer's prize.

Afterall, grace come in the evening of your struggles. God will not compete with your toiling and tireless effort. That's why grace comes at supper; when you are done with self-effort.

A survey of the Book of Revelation indicates that we have over a dozen references to the word overcome.

Here are some:

> (a) "To him that overcometh will I give to eat the fruit of life" (Rev. 2:7).
> (b) "He that overcometh shall not be hurt of the second death" (Rev. 2:11).
> (c) "To him that overcometh will I give to eat of the hidden manna" (Rev. 2:17).

(d) "And he that overcometh and keepeth my works unto the end, to him will I give power over the nation" (Rev. 2:26).

(e) He that overcometh, the same shall be clothed in white raiment" (Rev. 3:5).

(f) He that overcometh will I make a pillar in the temple of my God" (Rev. 3:12).

(g) To him that overcometh will I grant to sit with me in my throne, even as I also overcame" (Rev. 3:21).

(h) He that overcometh shall inherit all things, and I will be his God, and he shall be my son" (Rev. 21:7).

Jesus commission the overcomer

In Luke 10:19, Jesus gave you power. Hear Him. "Behold, I give unto you power to tread on serpents and scorpions, and over all the power of the enemy: and nothing shall by any means hurt you." Prior to the release of that power, Jesus had overcome the world for your sake. He says, "These things I have spoken unto you, that in me ye might have peace. In the world ye shall have tribulation: but be of good cheer; I have overcome the world" (John 16:33).

The significance of the scriptures above did not hit me until I began to follow the unfolding revolution which swept through the Arab world. It began in Tunisia sometimes in February of 2011. In no time, the Tunisian Government collapsed. Followed by that of Egypt. When the wind of change got to Libya, Gaddafi; the Libyan strongman refused to go; instead, he turned his gun on his people. Heavy armaments of war were in full display, bombing, killing, and chasing unarmed civilians. Gadhafi's army was on the verge of destroying Benghazi, the second largest city in Libya which has become the base for the opposition, when the world under the auspices of the United Nations voted overwhelmingly to enforce a no-fly zone over Libya.

An overnight aerial bombardment of Libya by the combined forces of the United States of America, France, and Britain changed the story. The world awoke the following morning to behold carcasses of tanks, vehicles, and other instruments of war, smoldering in smoke. In the words of a US general, "The capacity of Libya to respond to attacks were drastically degraded."

As I attempted to juxtapose the spectacle before me against the boastful words of one of Gaddafi's sons, a commander of the rapidly advancing forces, who warned the residents of Benghazi that "we are coming" it was at that moment that these scriptures began to play out like a movie in my mind.

Few days later, the tide changed. I watched in amazement, how the opposition; people who were hitherto running helplessly without guns were chasing back the otherwise dreaded Libyan army and taking strategic towns without hassles. What the UN achieved through its coalition was to overcome Col. Gaddafi, to the extent that the dreaded Libyan army lost its capacity to strike.

Jesus at Calvary drastically degraded the power of the enemy to harm you. The devil may still look like a giant but it has long lost its capacity to strike. The power that Jesus gave you in Luke 10:19 is a faith induced proactive power. It is for you to continually flip the switch and overrun the enemy. In the scripture Jesus mentioned two categories of power. "Behold, I give unto you power to tread on serpents and scorpions, and over all the power of the enemy: and nothing shall by any means hurt you."

The first which is highly potent is for you and forever at your disposal. The second is in reference to the degraded power of the enemy—the serpents and scorpions of your life. They are already in disguise while lying comatose. The power that Jesus gave to you is the very power that moves against your fear. That's why He charged you to "tread" or step on them. It is the power to destroy your phobia. The enemy may appear menacing but Jesus overcame him for you. Take that power and charge toward the enemy like the Libyan opposition and you will discover an enemy territory lying in wait to be possessed.

The proclamation of Jesus in Luke 10:19, expressly commissioned you an overcomer. That power is a gift from God. You didn't earn it like a college degree. Like every gift, it has to be received and appreciated. It has to be appreciated because Jesus paid the ultimate price with His precious blood. People are often not conscious of the magnitude of that gift and perhaps don't esteem it highly simply because it was a gift.

Expectedly, power goes with authority. As a believer, you are rooted and established in the covenant heritage of Christ hence you are a royal citizen of the kingdom family. You got the authority. Therefore step forward and exercise the power that goes with that authority. Through faith Christ made His home in your heart hence you were rooted and perfected in the love of Christ. "That Christ may dwell in your hearts by faith; that ye, being rooted and grounded in love" (Eph. 3:17).

In response to the commandment of God, Moses sent a reconnaissance team to the land of Canaan. The majority report was frightening. "And there we saw the giants, the sons of Anak, which come of the giants: and we were in our own sight as grasshoppers, and so we were in their sight" (Num. 13:33). They "were in their own sight as grasshoppers. "Put differently, they saw themselves through the mirror darkly and suffered from paranoia delusions." On the other hand, the minority report presented by Caleb was a demonstration of the exercise of the power that Jesus gave to you in Luke 10:19.

Listen to Caleb in Numbers 13:30. "And Caleb stilled the people before Moses, and said, Let us go up at once, and possess it; for we are well able to overcome it." God is giving you a testimony that he may change your grasshopper perspective. As soon as you catch the overcomer perspective, the exercise of your Kingdom authority becomes a pleasurable encounter. So shall it be in Jesus's name. Amen.

How to overcome. Revelation 12:11 says, "And they overcame him by the blood of the Lamb, and by the word of their testimony; and they loved not their lives unto the death." Without testimony, it is impossible to become an overcomer. God is in a hurry to give that undeniable experience which qualify you to join the ranks of Kingdom overcomers. Each time you recount your testimony, the overwhelming power of the Lord will prevail. The overcoming power resides in your testimony. To that end, it is not possible to overcome without going through the water and fire experience. God is continually looking for such an experience in you.

Conscious of that truth, Apostle James admonished us to "count it all joy when we enter into diverse temptation" (James 1:2). Stepping into diverse temptation is an accelerated route to becoming an overcomer. "Blessed is the man that endureth temptation: for when he is tried, he shall receive the crown of life, which the Lord hath promised to them that love him. Let no man say when he is tempted, I am tempted of God: for God cannot be tempted with evil, neither tempteth he any man" (James 1:12–13).

There's a crown to be received when you endure temptation. It is the overcomer crown. A number of things happen when you endure temptation. Confidences are bound to be shattered and uncertainty cleared. All your comfort zones are invaded and you will not be seen to be holding any more secrets before God. Thereafter, your journey of intimacy with God will gather momentum. At that level of intimacy, you are at liberty to proudly declare that you have overcome.

Revelation knowledge comes with intimacy with God. Toward the end of his excruciating ordeal, God engaged Job in a series of interrogative reasoning. Afterall He invited us to come let us reason together (Isa. 1:18). Since Job was unable to take up that divine challenge, God chose to enforce that invitation on the crest of the storm, which tormented Job.

GRACE IN HIS BOSOM

Chapters 38 through 42 are recorded accounts of that exchange. That exploded conversation brought Job to the point of intimacy with God. I must confess that the questions God posed to Job remain one of my most exciting passages of the Bible. Anytime, I wish to see what God of humor looks like, I will rush to Job 38. Those questions will humble you and in complete brokenness, you will notice that God is not a distant God. That's what happened to Job and ushered him to the point of intimacy with God. "Then Job answered the LORD, and said, I have heard of thee by the hearing of the ear: but now mine eye seeth thee" (Job 42:1, 5).

One tangible evidence of intimacy with God is when you can behold Him with the eye of your spirit. In Genesis 12:1, God spoke to Abram but in verse seven, the Lord appeared unto Abraham and "said". From that moment, Abram's journey of intimacy with God began. If God spoke to you, pray that He will appear to you. After Job saw the Lord with the eye of the Spirit, he spoke no more, instead he repented in "dust and ashes." Also, God spoke no more to Job for He had brought Job to the point of intimacy. In His awesomeness, God revealed Himself to an ignorant Job. What followed was celebration in heaven. Again, it was party time.

You are an overcomer because you left the devil behind. Your language has changed. Now, you are speaking the tongue language of heaven. Hallelujah has become your common refrain. Yea and amen, your body language. Truth is, the Holy Spirit doesn't reveal anything to angels. Satan being a fallen angel got no place close to revelation. No doubt, Satan understood every word of scripture. He even goes to church as we saw in the case of Job but glory to God that revelation knowledge is locked beyond the mesmerizing influence of the unemployed cherub. Albeit, the devil specializes in springing surprises.

However, when the Spirit of the Lord lifted up a standard, Isaiah 59:19, those flood of surprises, the tsunamis of your life are converted to rivers of living waters such that, henceforth, every droplet of water that you see is your latter rain. Latter rain is about the outpouring of the Holy Spirit to you, the saint of the Lord, so that you can effortlessly speak in tongues. "Be glad then, ye children of Zion, and rejoice in the LORD your God: for he hath given you the former rain moderately, and he will cause to come down for you the rain, the former rain, and the latter rain in the first month" (Joel 2:23). It's a season of fresh outpouring of the Holy Spirit upon you. Rejoice and be glad.

While the enemy is going to and fro and walking up and down the earth, looking for whom he may devour; the eye of the Lord runs (scan) to and fro the earth to distinguish you—the one whose heart is set on Him. "And the LORD said unto Satan, Whence comest thou? Then Satan answered the LORD, and said, From going to and fro in the earth, and from walking up and down in it" (Job 1:7). Same question was repeated in Job 2:2 and the answer remained the same. Second Chronicles 16:9 says, "For the eyes of the LORD run to and fro throughout the whole earth, to shew himself strong in the behalf of them whose heart is perfect toward him. Herein thou hast done foolishly: therefore from henceforth thou shalt have wars."

Jesus overcame for you. His precious blood saved you. Everything about you is in Christ. Consequently, He declared, "Ye are of God, little children and have overcome them: because greater is he that is in you than he that is in the world" (1 John 4:4). Christ in you, the hope of glory (Col. 1:27).

His processing chambers

God's processing chamber is tribulation. Granted, God is not the author of confusion and will never put you through hardship. Nonetheless whatever the devil meant for bad in your life, God turns it for good. That's why Jesus divinely embeds Himself in every storm that comes your way. In John 16:33, He says, "These things I have spoken unto you, that in me ye might have peace. In the world ye shall have tribulation: but be of good cheer; I have overcome the world." Notice that Christ didn't say that you would not go through tribulation, instead He said in doing so that you must be of good cheer because He has overcome the world. Tribulation is a subset of evil and devilish events in the world. If Christ overcame the whole, which is the entire world; how much more microscopic challenges and circumstances that are dominant in the world.

Put differently, Christ already neutralizes and owns every tribulation in the world and has turned them into God's processing chambers. Precious metals like gold and silver don't come easy. To glitter, they must undergo processing through the fire furnace. God permits that you get through His processing chamber in order to get a yes out of you. Mary said yes without hesitation. "And Mary said, Behold the handmaid of the Lord; be it unto me according to thy word. And the angel departed from her" (Luke 1:38). With Jonah it was different. God put Jonah through His processing chamber until He got a yes. "Now the LORD had prepared a great fish to swallow up Jonah. And Jonah was in the belly of the fish three days and three nights" (Jonah 1:17).

After three days in the processing chamber, Jonah raced to Nineveh in the speed of Elijah, for his God given assignment. Tribulation works patience. Many a saint fail to heed the call of God until we are in the midst of crises. In such situations, God pulls back the veil of our humanity, so that we can grasp the depth of His unfailing love and compassion.

Moses was a graduate of the processing chamber. The chamber is a process because it consists of segments which are linked together but largely intangible. At the core of that process is learning how to trust God. David walked through the "shadow of death" yet he was never fearful. The shadow of death represents discouragement and hopelessness. God's plan for your life requires faith. "But without faith it is impossible to please God" (Heb. 11:16). Your faith must be tried. "That the trial of your faith, being much more precious than of gold that perisheth, though it be tried with fire, might be found unto praise and honour and glory at the appearing of Jesus Christ" (1 Peter 1:7). Life is in the furnace of the fire of tough times. You go into the furnace, you come out strong but humble. Most importantly, you come out alive to Christ.

GRACE IN HIS BOSOM

Consider the story of the three Hebrew men thrown into the furnace. The King saw four men instead of three. "He answered and said, Lo, I see four men loose, walking in the midst of the fire, and they have no hurt; and the form of the fourth is like the Son of God" (Dan. 3:25). The fourth is Jesus. Jesus is still in the furnace. He is Lord over all the elements that constitute the storm of your life.

Beyond worship. Beyond worship is the love of God. Love is the amalgamation and crystallization of worship. Love is all the activity of worship rolled together. That's why it is the foremost and great commandment. Love is the epitome of worship. When the Pharisee asked Jesus, "Master, which is the great commandment in the law? Jesus said unto him, Thou shalt love the Lord thy God with all thy heart, and with all thy soul, and with all thy mind. This is the first and great commandment" (Matt. 22:36–38).

The knowledge of God, that you acquire is expected to transform to the love of God. When the measurement of the man of Ezekiel 47, reached the fourth level, "and it was a river that I could not pass over: for the waters were risen, waters to swim in, a river that could not be passed over." At that remarkable level, it is expected that you are filled with the love of God. Beyond knowledge and worship is love. Worship provokes power whereas power is wrapped in love.

Expounding the parable of the sower, Jesus says, "And these are they likewise which are sown on stony ground; who, when they have heard the word, immediately receive it with gladness; And have no root in themselves, and so endure but for a time: afterward, when affliction or persecution ariseth for the word's sake, immediately they are offended" (Mark 4:16–17). The "root" in reference is love. If you have no root in yourself, that implies that you are without the love of God.

Ephesians 3:17–19 emphasized, "That Christ may dwell in your hearts by faith; that ye, being rooted and grounded in love, May be able to comprehend with all saints what is the breadth, and length, and depth, and height; And to know the love of Christ, which passeth knowledge, that ye might be filled with all the fulness of God." Knowledge is to take you to the love of Christ. Love is the ultimate destination of Kingdom knowledge. It is not possible to be "rooted and grounded in love" until you get to the river level of knowledge and worship. Rivers have breadth, length, depth, and height. At that level, together with other swimmers, you may be able to comprehend the common field of experience in Christ-which is love.

All power in love

God's call and choice is not without power. The power is borne out of knowledge and encapsulated in love.

> According as his divine power hath given unto us all things that pertain unto life and godliness, through the knowledge of him that hath called us to glory and virtue: Whereby are given unto us exceeding great and precious promises: that by these ye might be partakers of the divine nature,

GRACE IN HIS BOSOM

> having escaped the corruption that is in the world through lust. And beside this, giving all diligence, add to your faith virtue; and to virtue knowledge; And to knowledge temperance; and to temperance patience; and to patience godliness; And to godliness brotherly kindness; and to brotherly kindness charity. For if these things be in you, and abound, they make you that ye shall neither be barren nor unfruitful in the knowledge of our Lord Jesus Christ. But he that lacketh these things is blind, and cannot see afar off, and hath forgotten that he was purged from his old sins. Wherefore the rather, brethren, give diligence to make your calling and election sure: for if ye do these things, ye shall never fall. (1 Pet. 1:3–10)

It starts with faith, then worship and ends in love. Love is the divine nature and that is your Kingdom destination. Anyone who is insufficient in love is devoid of the cumulation of our common experience in Christ. Ephesians 4:15–16 submit, "But speaking the truth in love, may grow up into him in all things, which is the head, even Christ: From whom the whole body fitly joined together and compacted by that which every joint supplieth, according to the effectual working in the measure of every part, maketh increase of the body unto the edifying of itself in love." Your strength as a believer is rooted in love. When you attain the love zone, you shall no longer be like a child, tossed by the waves and blown about by the wind of the doctrine of deceitful men who led others astray by tricks (Eph. 4:4).

Communication

"Yea, if thou criest after knowledge, and liftest up thy voice for understanding" (Prov. 2:3).

Notice that the voice is lifted only for understanding and not for wisdom. That is significant. A separation seems to have taken place. The voice accounts for the separation. If you grasp that truth, you have availed yourself with the most important phenomenon or distinguishing feature between the process of getting wisdom and that of understanding.

In a nutshell, communication is a process by which information is transferred from person, place to another. By process it means that the operation is continuous, largely intangible and follows certain steps that are sequentially arranged.

The basic elements of all communication are the same, though there might be slight differences. These elements include the source or sender, receiver, message, and the channel or medium. Other factors are feedback, which is the response given by the receiver and noise. Noise or distortion is anything that subtracts from the vibrancy of the message. In human communication, these elements are inseparable.

Communication ensures that your relationship with God assumes a more practical dimension. God, the Source spoke first. If you read the Bible, that suggests that you received the open message from God the encoder. Essentially, you reacted on the basis of that message to acquire the knowledge about God and His Kingdom. In response to the message, "You lift up your voice for understanding."

Communication is a two-way affair. Without your response, communication cannot be said to have occurred. For communication to take place, there must be a speaker and a listener; a sender and a receiver; an encoder and a decoder. God in His majestic sovereignty, spoke first, outside of time. Your response is a confirmation that you received the message and reacted accordingly. Your response may be in the form of enquiry, prayer, or petition. Your response is wrapped up in one word: obedience. The journey of understanding begins at the stage of communication.

Shared meaning

That stage represents a watershed. Truth is, communication do not happen when the message is received, rather communication takes place when there is a shared meaning. The quest for a shared meaning is the breeding place of intimacy. Understanding is wrought when there is a shared meaning. Shared meaning take the form of divine insight or revelation. The commonality of the sharing of the field of experience between God (The Source) and you (The receiver) is central to divine communication.

The Bible as a book qualifies to be ranked as a means of communication. It is a book that communicates God's words to His sons and daughters. The message communicated is primarily verbal.

There is no idle word in the Bible. It might be of interest at this point to understand why God chose the words He used. Were His words based upon a criterion of meaning? How does the meaning of God's word relate to your purpose on earth? Do you wish to ascribe meaning to the Word of God in relation to your needs or for His purpose? What is the purpose of the Bible message?

Understanding of purpose is critical to how you receive the message and react to the message because purpose ignites passion. Lastly, you must be willing to communicate, to ask questions and receive answers.

First Timothy 6:18 says, "That they do good, that they be rich in good works, ready to distribute, willing to communicate." God is a God of order. You may not see the different processes that constitute what is known as communication but everything done by God is arranged in a manner to help you receive it without inhibitions.

There is always a parallel between the things that happen in the earthly environment with those that occur in heavenly or spiritual realms. The communication process is in stages: ideation, encoding, transmission, reception, and encoding. The whole idea of a Kingdom belongs to God. He encoded His purposes, commandments, instructions, and promises in words and transmitted them openly to His offspring on earth. Sequel to that, it is the responsibility of His offspring as receivers of the message to decode what

God encoded and ensure clear reception, and most importantly the expected feedback.

It is important, therefore, not only to learn the language of the Kingdom but to have a good knowledge of the King and His kingdom.

Sharp Spiritual antenna. That is why intimacy with self is a condition for intimacy with God. Intimacy with self permits you to sharpen your spiritual antennae, ready to pick up signals from heaven. As soon as you begin to respond to the messages received from God, you assume the role of a sender. When you praise, worship, or pray, God always responds with revelations and insights. If your spirit man is not sensitive, you run the risk of missing out on the message. That's a tragedy. The Sender has no problem. The problem has always been with man, the receiver and frictions dominant in the visible world.

Man as the receiver

The receiver or decoder is one that receives the message. He is expected to decode the message and respond accordingly. He is expected to receive the message in the order the encoder encodes it. In human communication, oftentimes the message is not received with clarity due to distortions.

The other name for distortions is noise and noise can occur at any stage of the communication process. With God it is not so. There is neither noise around the divine Source nor within the channel—Holy Spirit. The Source, the message the channel are one. It is Light and life. "But all things that are reproved are made manifest by the light: for whatsoever doth make manifest is light" (Eph. 5:13).

Noise represents darkness. Light and darkness cannot dwell together. To receive clear signals from radio, for instance, the antenna must be properly positioned. In a similar manner, that part in man (spirit) that bears witness with the Spirit of God is expected to be sharp and sensitive.

God the source

We are amply aware that God is the Source of everything here on earth and beyond. That is why He is known as God the Creator, the Almighty God. Nonetheless, in the context of communication, we are looking at God as the encoder or sender of a message. God encoded all that He wanted us to know in a book called the Bible. He spoke through prophets and messengers via the inspiration of the Holy Spirit to us. Speaking through forty mail runners and oracles and in sixty-six books, the Bible became a compendium of God's words to man. God still speaks to us even unto this day.

Generally, the source is the initiator of the message acting for himself or on behalf of someone or organization. God is the Supreme initiator, the divine encoder of His message as recorded in the Bible to His kingdom community on earth. That message is in the form of promises, instructions, commandments, which touch every facet of our lives on earth. God expect you to receive the message (His words) and clasp them in your heart. He is aware that a time will come when you will begin to respond. In all, the sender sets the order in which the receiver is expected to receive the message.

Holy Spirit as channel

The channel is also known as medium. It is the medium or channel through which the message is received by the decoder. God is a Spirit and they that worship Him must do so in spirit and in truth. Granted, the Bible is a book but it will be wrong to refer to the book as the channel by which we receive the Word of God.

The Word of God is received by men through the channel of the Holy Spirit. The Word of God is shared in the hearts of men by the Holy Spirit.

The Bible was written by men through the inspiration of the Holy Spirit hence the Holy Spirit is the channel and the medium all rolled together. He is the conveyor of God's word to you the receiver. The Holy Spirit is the divine link between you and God. He brings God's words to us and takes our response back to God. That is how He intercedes for us with groaning that can hardly be uttered.

In mass communication, the medium is often a structure, an organ, visible and identifiable such as radio and television. The Holy Spirit is a personality, though not visible per se but you can feel the presence, the outpouring of the spirit.

The channel in which signals travels must be in good condition to ensure clarity of reception. Interruptions of any sort which interferes in the process of communication, with a view to distorting the content of the message is referred to as noise.

Perception

On a broad outline, spiritual communication revolves around the following: (a) perception, (b) on knowledge, (c) on experience. Perception is a constructive process. It has to do with the significance of the information concerned. Perception takes place when there is an interplay of more than one sensory organ leading to a combination of sensations into a recognition.

Perception plays a vital role in interpreting spiritual signals. As you begin to seek Him, your spiritual antennae is sharpened to the extent that you can pick spiritual signals without hesitation. Such spiritual signals are borne out of the threshold of a robust knowledge base and shared experience.

In the preceding chapters, we discussed the importance of knowledge and the need for a shared experience in Christ. Those two elements are necessary toward a rich perceptive ability. If the atmosphere is right, spiritual signals flow like streams, in slides and images. Perception is of the heart just as the Word of God.

Moses told the children of Israel, "Yet the Lord hath not given you an heart to perceive, an eyes to see, and ears to hear, unto this day" (Deut. 29:4).

Nonetheless, the Shunammite woman had a different experience. It was perception that opened her door of blessing. Hear what she narrated to her husband. "And she said unto her husband; Behold now, I perceive that this is an holy man of God, which passeth by us continually" (2

Kings 4:9). The spiritual signal registered as sensation in her heart with a strong nudging that led to recognition.

As soon as you perceive, you are persuaded to verbalize or say what the Holy Spirit lays in your heart. Both perception and understanding have a strong link. They belong to the heart. The implication is that these two important elements are taken beyond the sensory organs. They find expressions in the heart of man. Your inability to perceive is a strong signal of spiritual ineptitude. Make no excuses about it.

In Matthew 13:13–14, Jesus pointed out the kernel of the discussion. "Therefore speak I to them in parables: because they seeing see not; and hearing they hear not, neither do they understand. And in them is fulfilled the prophecy of Esaias, which saith, By hearing ye shall hear, and shall not understand; and seeing ye shall see, and shall not perceive." When the woman with the issue of blood touched the hem of Jesus's garment, none of those around Him noticed it. "And Jesus said, somebody hath touched me: for I perceive that virtue is gone out of me" (Luke 8:46). Jesus perceived that power was gone out of Him.

Peter perceived that God is no respecter of persons (Acts 10:34). With perception come conviction and persuasion. Paul perceived that their journey would be with hurt and much damage (Acts 27:10). Certain events or occurrences could lead to perception as was the case with Joshua and Eleazer the priest in Joshua 22:31. "And Phinehas the son of Eleazar the priest said unto the children of Reuben, and to the children of Gad, and to the children of Manasseh, This day we perceive that the LORD is among us, because ye have not committed this trespass against the LORD: now ye have delivered the children of Israel out of the hand of the LORD." Both perceived the strong presence of the Lord. Their perception was borne out of experience and robust knowledge of God.

On the other hand, Job confessed that in two instances, he could not perceive the presence of God. "Lo, he goeth by me, and I see him not: he passeth on also, but I perceive him not" (Job 9:11). The story of Job is a lesson in perception. A man God described as a perfect and upright man. Job, a man that was in the habit of sanctifying for perceived sin, a sacred duty he was not chosen to perform; could not in the least perceive the presence of God. Also, God made a hedge about him and his household yet he couldn't perceive the overwhelming presence of God round about him. Little wonder that while the exchange was going on between God and Satan over his (Job) glorious destiny, he couldn't perceive also. Could it be that Job lived by assumption?

Was he never persuaded and convinced that God was with him? Job was a just and perfect man who didn't know the God that he feared. "Behold, I go forward but he is not there; and backward, but I cannot perceive him" (Job 23:8). Job did everything that God recognizes as good on earth but he doesn't have the knowledge of God. For lack of knowledge, Job suffered. He couldn't discern spiritual signals because wisdom was absent.

Throughout the Book of Job, his anguish complaints were predicated on the seemingly absence of knowledge, wisdom and understanding. Job didn't know how and where to locate those treasures but he was convinced they were gifts from God. Job couldn't perceive because his relationship with God was short of intimacy.

No doubt, Job was very religious but he didn't know God. Put differently, Job was not in covenant with God. God referred to Job as "my servant" (Job 1:8) because his good deeds "are come up for a memorial before God" (Acts 16:4). God honors faith even when it is ill motivated. I perceive that Job broke a hedge because of ignorance.

In his ignorance, he tried to set the rules for his relationship with God. Satan was aware that God made a hedge about Job and his house, and about all that he hath on every side (Job 1:10). However, Job was not aware of that because revelation knowledge was not imparted to him. Revelation is a product of intimacy.

Truth is, revelation doesn't precede the word. God set His rules. He says receive my word first. You must know what God says about Himself and His Kingdom. There is no circumvention or shortcuts when it comes to knowing God. Any attempt to approach God in any other way is tantamount to breaking a hedge. Expectedly,

"He that diggeth a pit shall fall into it; and whosoever breaketh an hedge, a serpent shall bite him" (Eccl. 10:8). Look around and you will notice so many Jobs. Good people who help the needy and the poor. They provide for the orphans and the widows. They are beacons of hope in their communities. In their ignorance they erroneously believe that their good deeds will make up for their lack of personal relationship with God. Expectedly, God will build hedges around them and bless them because their good

GRACE IN HIS BOSOM

deeds continue to reach God as a memorial (Acts 10:4). Remind such persons of kingdom service in the house of God or payment of tithes and offerings; they are quick to point at their good works. Like Job, they are perfect and upright but they lack knowledge.

Notwithstanding, Satan has not ceased going to church. There are three reasons why Satan goes to the house of the Lord. First is to prevent you from giving your life to Christ. The devil doesn't want you to respond to the altar call. Second is to prevent you from giving tithe and offering. Lastly is to obtain permission from God to punish such as the "perfect and upright" of our society.

Why will God allow bad things to happen to good people? The answer is simple: that they may know Him. Job the author of "my Redeemer liveth" didn't truly know his Redeemer. Job couldn't perceive the time of His visitation. Job confessed, "Lo, he goeth by me and I see him not: he passeth on also, but I perceive him not." The situation Job found himself was indeed lamentable. He couldn't perceive that the accuser of the brethren had raised the red flag before God. Most importantly, he failed to understand the time of His visitation.

Recall that Jesus wept over Jerusalem because they didn't know the time of their visitation.

> And when he was come near, he beheld the city, and wept over it, Saying, If thou hadst known, even thou, at least in this thy day, the things which belong unto thy peace! but now they are hid from thine

eyes. For the days shall come upon thee, that thine enemies shall cast a trench about thee, and compass thee round, and keep thee in on every side, And shall lay thee even with the ground, and thy children within thee; and they shall not leave in thee one stone upon another; because thou knewest not the time of thy visitation. (Luke 19:41–44)

It is a serious matter when things that belong to your peace! are hidden from you simply because you are unaware of the time of your visitation. If the above scripture is not a picture of what came upon the man Job, I don't know where else in the Bible that we could obtain a portrait of the magnitude of disaster that befell Job. Unaware of the time of your visitation is a symptom of a lopsided relationship.

In Luke 22, Jesus alerted Peter when the enemy came for him. "And the Lord said, Simon, Simon, behold, Satan hath desired to have you, that he may sift you as wheat: But I have prayed for thee, that thy faith fail not: and when thou art converted, strengthen thy brethren" (Luke 22:31–32). Why was Job not alerted or warned as was the case with Peter?

Conversation is the seed of understanding

Jesus alerted Peter of the impending danger. Peter knew the Messiah and was always in conversation with Him. Conversation is a critical element of intimacy. Were

GRACE IN HIS BOSOM

it not for Peter's inquisitions, the many important tenets of our faith would have remained a mystery. Conversation is the seed of understanding.

On the other hand, there was no instance throughout the Book of Job prior to chapter 38, when the voice of God thundered like a whirlwind; where it was recorded that the man Job reasoned with God. In fact, he was afraid to do so. Job was not even in church the day when the sons of God came to present themselves before the Lord and Satan came also among them (Job 1:6).

Listen to Job. "How much less shall I answer him, and choose out my words to reason with him? Whom, though I were righteous, yet would I not answer, but I would make supplication to my judge. If I had called, and he had answered me; yet would I not believe that he had hearkened unto my voice" (Job 9:14–16). Job understands that his Redeemer lives but was obviously unaware of the ways of God.

"He made known his ways unto Moses, his acts unto the children of Israel" (Ps. 103:7). David cried, "Teach me thy way, O LORD, and lead me in a plain path, because of mine enemies" (Ps. 27:11).

As you study the Word of God, it is imperative to recognize the principles of God vis-a-vis His purposes. God's principles are His way. They don't change. They will produce the same result anywhere under heaven.

Interestingly, Job didn't know where to find God. Eliphaz, the Temanite, one of his three friends had admonished him. "Acquaint now thyself with him, and be at peace: thereby good shall come unto thee. Receive, I pray thee, the law from his mouth and lay up his words in thine heart" (Job 22:21–22). In response Job said, "Oh that I knew where I might find him! that I might come even to his seat!" (Job 23:3).

The scripture in Psalm 22:3 says that God inhabits the praises of His people. Job was a man without praise. There was no record that he praised God in the manner of David or Paul and Silas or in any manner whatsoever.

Distraction

Martha was distracted. In communication, anything that subtracts from the vibrancy of the message is collectively known as noise. In a similar manner, anything that takes away your focus from Christ constitutes a *noisome pestilence*. The one word for it is *distraction*.

Distraction simply means to be overly occupied with things or, better still, to be drawn away.

"Now it came to pass, as they went, that he entered into a certain village: and a certain woman named Martha received him into her house. And she had a sister called Mary, which also sat at Jesus' feet, and heard his word. But Martha was cumbered about much serving, and came to him, and said, Lord, dost thou not care that my sister hath left me to serve alone? bid her therefore that she help me. And Jesus answered and said unto her, Martha, Martha, thou art careful and troubled about many things: But one thing is needful: and Mary hath chosen that good part, which shall not be taken away from her." (Luke 10:38–42)

Another version puts it pointedly, "But Martha was distracted."

Martha was occupied and drawn away at the same time. That's tantamount to a total eclipse of attention to which a deficit was accounted for her. In a busy world such as ours, so many things compete for your attention. That's not new. It has always been so over the ages. However, with the advent of modern computer technology, especially the handsets that have the tendency to draw the users away from the crowd per se and create the unique aura of privacy, it's increasingly difficult for the believer to remain focused.

The loser appears to be time, but in an actual sense, it is the individual who lost everything including time for devotion, time for studying the Word of God, time for preaching and evangelism, and time for praying for lost souls. Indeed, those are the times for those things that we can't do in heaven. The scripture enjoined us to redeem time. "Walk in wisdom toward them that are without, redeeming the time" (Col. 4:5).

Prior to taking Jesus on a pinnacle of the temple, the devil took him up into a high mountain, shewed unto him all the kingdoms of the world in a moment of time. "And the devil, taking him up into an high mountain, shewed unto him all the kingdoms of the world in a moment of time. And the devil said unto him, All this power will I give thee, and the glory of them: for that is delivered unto me; and to whomsoever I will I give it" (Luke 4:5–6).

The Kingdoms of the world and the glory of them represent distractions. To serve God, you must turn your back to the distractions of the world. The kingdoms of the world doesn't glorify God. That's why He wants His Kingdom come and His will be done on earth. There has to be a separation because you as a vessel have to be clean and empty. Moses said, "I will turn aside" (Exod. 3:3). Elisha told the widow of Zeraphath, "Shut the door upon thee and upon thy sons" (2 Kings 4:4). That's separation. You have to shut the doors on relationships and things of this world which doesn't glorify God. Separate yourself from those things that distract and drain you. First Corinthians 6:19–20 puts it succinctly. "What? know ye not that your body is the temple of the Holy Ghost which is in you, which ye have of God, and ye are not your own? For ye are bought with a price: therefore glorify God in your body, and in your spirit, which are God's."

The devil is a corruption of anything that glorifies God. He doesn't want you to hear the voice of the Lord hence he introduced noise. Noise is a distraction. For your glorious destiny to be aborted, you must first be distracted. Jesus refused to be distracted. You too must not be distracted if the perfect will of God must be fulfilled in your life.

Distraction is a major enemy of your spiritual walk with God. Distraction happens in a diverse manner. They fall into two broad categories: worry and sin. Martha was worried, troubled, and evidently unhappy with her younger sister, Mary. But Mary chose devotion to the Word over much serving. It's possible that Mary, after listening to Jesus, might have helped Martha with service. Nonetheless, Mary chose the *one thing* that was needful when it mattered most. It's dangerous to be in church and be busy with other things while the Word is being preached. The Word is the only reason why you are in church in the first instance. You should prioritize the hearing of the Word over every other thing.

To mitigate against worry is not necessarily about prudent time management but priority. Christ is to be prioritized and valued over every other thing.

"Be still, and know that I am God: I will be exalted among the heathen, I will be exalted in the earth" (Ps. 46:10). At the feet of Jesus, Mary was still. If you are overly distracted and preoccupied with other things, then your ears will not hear the *still small voice*. The still small voice doesn't come amidst noisome worries. It resonates after the earthquake and fire.

"And he said, "Go forth, and stand upon the mount before the Lord. And, behold, the Lord passed by, and a great and strong wind rent the mountains, and brake in pieces the rocks before the LORD; but the Lord was not in the wind: and after the wind an earthquake; but the Lord was not in the earthquake: And after the earthquake a fire; but the Lord was not in the fire: and after the fire a still small voice. And it was so, when Elijah heard it, that he wrapped his face in his mantle, and went out, and stood in the entering in of the cave. And, behold, there came a voice unto him, and said, What doest thou here, Elijah?" (1 Kgs. 19:11–13)

Synonyms of distraction include diversion, interruption, disturbance, intrusion, interference, obstruction, frenzy, hysteria, madness, insanity, wilderness, and mania. A cursory look at the synonyms suggests an ascending order of distraction to the point of wilderness and mania experience. That's how low the abyss that distraction can take its victim to the point of wilderness and mania experience. But you are exempted in Jesus's name.

Common distractions include your everyday worries and your hectic routine and commitments.

Jesus meets your need

According to psychologists, there are three basic needs of man, namely food, clothing, and shelter. Anything you desire outside of these basic needs constitutes a *want*. The good news is that you can survive without wanting. Addressing the futility of worrying, Jesus spoke to His disciples in this manner.

"And he said unto his disciples, Therefore I say unto you, Take no thought for your life, what ye shall eat; neither for the body, what ye shall put on. The life is more than meat, and the body is more than raiment. Consider the ravens: for they neither sow nor reap; which neither have storehouse nor barn; and God feedeth them: how much more are ye better than the fowls? And which of you with taking thought can add to his stature one cubit? If ye then be not able to do that thing which is least, why take ye thought for the rest? Consider the lilies how they grow: they toil not, they spin not; and yet I say unto you, that Solomon in all his glory was not arrayed like one of these. If then God so clothe the grass, which is to day in the field, and to morrow is cast into the oven; how much more will he clothe you, O ye of little faith? And seek not ye what ye shall eat, or what ye shall drink, neither be ye of doubtful mind. For all these things do the nations of the world seek after: and your Father knoweth that ye have need of these things. But rather seek ye the kingdom of God; and all these things shall be added unto you. Fear not, little flock; for it is your Father's good pleasure to give you the kingdom. (Luke 12:22–32)

Happily, none of us can add one cubit unto our stature by taking thoughts hostage. Martha was encumbered. Truth is, there's no place for encumbrances if you must follow Jesus. He says, "Follow me and I will make you" (Matt. 4:17). If you must follow Jesus, burdensome kinds of stuff such as thoughts about tomorrow must vacate your mind and make way for trust. Every provision that you desire is resident in your trust and obedience. Worry is fueled by your fervent desire to serve tomorrow. "Take therefore no thought for the morrow: for the morrow shall take thought for the things of itself. Sufficient unto the day is the evil thereof" (Matt. 6:34).

Rich distract. It's easy for the rich to be distracted. Consider the parable of the great supper.

"Then said he unto him, A certain man made a great supper, and bade many: And sent his servant at supper time to say to them that were bidden, Come; for all things are now ready. And they all with one consent began to make excuse. The first said unto him, I have bought a piece of ground, and I must needs go and see it: I pray thee have me excused. And another said, I have bought five yoke of oxen, and I go to prove them: I pray thee have me excused. And another said, I have married a wife, and therefore I cannot come. So that servant came, and shewed his lord these things. Then the master of the house being angry said to his servant, Go out quickly into the streets and lanes of the city, and bring in hither the poor, and the maimed, and the halt, and the blind. And the servant said, Lord, it is done as thou hast commanded, and yet there is room. And the Lord said unto the servant, Go out into the highways and hedges, and compel them to come in, that my house may be filled. For I say unto you, That none of those men which were bidden shall taste of my supper. (Luke 14:16–24)

The rich were honorably invited, but due to worries about their possessions, they all declined in quick succession, providing a range of excuses. The one that got married cited his marriage as an excuse not to attend. Marriage is a great and honorable union instituted by God. It is right to reason that the newly wedded would be proud to go to the diner in the company of his lovely wife. But that wasn't the case as they all missed out on the kingdom banquet due to the burden imposed by riches in the likeness of worries. In Mark 9:21, Jesus asked the young rich man who claimed to be perfect to go and sell his possessions and give the proceeds to the poor but he was offended.

Greed distract. Gehazi was in line for succession, but he was distracted. After Naaman was healed of leprosy via the instrumentality of Prophet Elisha, the prophet rejected all entreaties to be blessed by the Syrian captain. Nonetheless, Gehazi, the servant of the prophet, thought he was wiser than his master. Hear him.

"But Gehazi, the servant of Elisha the man of God, said, Behold, my master hath spared Naaman this Syrian, in not receiving at his hands that which he brought: but, as the Lord liveth, I will run after him, and take somewhat of him. (2 Kgs. 5:20)

So it was that Gehazi followed after Naaman and collected two talents of silver in two bags with two changes of garment and "bestowed them in the house" on his return. When the prophet confronted him, he claimed not to have left his immediate vicinity unknown to him that the man of God captured the entire exchange between him and Naaman in the spirit.

"And he said unto him, Went not mine heart with thee, when the man turned again from his chariot to meet thee? Is it a time to receive money, and to receive garments, and oliveyards, and vineyards, and sheep, and oxen, and menservants, and maidservants? The leprosy therefore of Naaman shall cleave unto thee, and unto thy seed for ever. And he went out from his presence a leper as white as snow. (2 Kgs. 5:26–27)

Flesh distract. A consortium of things are lying in wait to distract the believer from his glorious kingdom journey. Flesh distracted Samson. He was a man of enormous strength and courage but was knocked out of alignment with the Holy Spirit because of the love for women in the enemy camp. Consequently, the Spirit of the Lord departed from him, but he was unaware. Listen to his prayer.

"And Samson called unto the Lord, and said, O Lord God, remember me, I pray thee, and strengthen me, I pray thee, only this once, O God, that I may be at once avenged of the Philistines for my two eyes. (Judg. 16:28)

The prodigal brother in Luke 15 was distracted by self-righteousness and unforgiveness. In Esther 1:12, Queen Vashti was distracted by disobedience. "But the queen Vashti refused to come at the king's commandment

GRACE IN HIS BOSOM

by his chamberlains: therefore was the king very wroth, and his anger burned in him."

In 1 Samuel 2, the children of Eli were grossly distracted. They were scoundrels for they treated the Lord's offering with contempt. Additionally, they seduced the young woman who assisted at the entrance of the tabernacle.

Also, anger distracts as well as murmuring and gossiping.

Dangers of worrying

Prominent among the dangers posed by worrying is the tendency to obstruct the gospel.

"He also that received seed among the thorns is he that heareth the word; and the care of this world, and the deceitfulness of riches, choke the word, and he becometh unfruitful. But he that received seed into the good ground is he that heareth the word, and understandeth it; which also beareth fruit, and bringeth forth, some an hundredfold, some sixty, some thirty. (Matt. 13:22–23)

In worrying is the care of this world made manifest. The deceitfulness of riches lures the believer into a state of frenetic and unnecessary vibrations in the spirit man, which in turn facilitates the choking of the word. The result is unfruitfulness for the brethren. "No man that warreth entangleth himself with the affairs of this life; that he may please him who hath chosen him to be a soldier" (2 Tim. 2:4). For that reason, worrying is not to be associated with the believer. As a soldier of Christ, you are part of the church militant on earth.

The greatest desire of any soldier is to remain obedient to his commander. No soldier achieves that should he choose to entangle himself with the affairs of the world. Jesus asked you to consider the ravens. The ravens possess a singular quality, which distinguished them from other species. That quality is known as *least concern*. What that means is that the ravens are *least concerned* about what goes on around them. In that manner, the ravens can't be distracted by anything simply because they are *least concerned*. If the believer must not be distracted, you must emulate the ravens in the exercise of the quality of being least concerned. That way, nothing will offend you. You can't be tempted unless you are drawn away. Put differently, the devil can't get you except when you are distracted. Do not err, brethren.

"Let no man say when he is tempted, I am tempted of God: for God cannot be tempted with evil, neither tempteth he any man: But every man is tempted, when he is drawn away of his own lust, and enticed. Then when lust hath conceived, it bringeth forth sin: and sin, when it is finished, bringeth forth death. Do not err, my beloved brethren. (Jas. 1:13–16)

Consequences of worry. The consequences of worrying are summed up in one word, *death*.

"For to be carnally minded is death; but to be spiritually minded is life and peace. Because the carnal mind is enmity against God: for it is not subject to the law of God, neither indeed can be. So then they that are in the flesh cannot please God. (Rom. 8:6–8)

Carnality of the mind connotes spiritual death, which is a sure way to natural death. When the mind is corrupted, the soul dies. Ditto the spirit. The mind and the spirit are in union to give life to the soul. A carnal soul is a miserable soul. On the other hand, spiritual mindedness is eternal life. A life of peace and comfort springs from a sanctified soul. "For he that soweth to his flesh shall of the flesh reap corruption; but he that soweth to the Spirit shall of the Spirit reap life everlasting" (Gal. 6:8).

Psalm 39:6 points to worry as vanity. "Surely every man walketh in a vain shew: surely they are disquieted in vain: he heapeth up riches, and knoweth not who shall gather them." We worry, we fret, we vex, we toil, and we care, heaping up riches without an assurance of who shall gather them after we're done with our occupation on earth. That's indeed vanity. Manure, which is rich in nutrients, fertilizes the soil. No matter its usefulness, it's useless when it's heaped in the field without spreading.

How to mitigate distraction

Jesus issued a warning against distraction and against worrying. It's more of a command. Hear Him.

"And take heed to yourselves, lest at any time your hearts be overcharged with surfeiting, and drunkenness, and cares of this life, and so that day come upon you unawares. For as a snare shall it come on all them that dwell on the face of the whole earth. Watch ye therefore, and pray always, that ye may be accounted worthy to escape all these things that shall come to pass, and to stand before the Son of man." (Luke 21:34–36)

The scripture emphasizes the need to guard your heart with all diligence against overcharge. A generous caution against sin and anxiety must be exercised over your own soul. Due largely to the inordinate pursuit of the comforts of this world, the heart is overcharged. The result is a nest of ensnarement in wait for the frenetic busy heart.

Aware of our rumbling for the care of the world, Jesus adequately admonished us.

"Therefore I say unto you, Take no thought for your life, what ye shall eat, or what ye shall drink; nor yet for your body, what ye shall put on. Is not the life more than meat, and the body than raiment? (Matt. 6:25)

Again, in John 6:27, Jesus says,

"Labour not for the meat which perisheth, but for that meat which endureth unto everlasting life, which the Son of man shall give unto you: for him hath God the Father sealed.

"The summation of the scriptures above is that seeking earthly things first over the things of the kingdom must be considered a forbidden desire. "But seek ye first the kingdom of God, and his righteousness; and all these things shall be added unto you" (Matt. 6:33). Everything you desire in the kingdom revolves around seeking the kingdom as a matter of priority. Seeking first the kingdom of God and its righteousness introduces you to the fundamentals of Christianity as a way of life. It puts anxiety and worrying far from you as you will begin to hear clearly from the Lord.

The pathway. Addressing the issue of marriage and women, Apostle Paul in 1 Corinthians 7:32–35 further pointed us to a pathway toward a life devoid of worries and distraction.

"But I would have you without carefulness. He that is unmarried careth for the things that belong to the Lord, how he may please the Lord: But he that is married careth for the things that are of the world, how he may please his wife. There is difference also between a wife and a virgin. The unmarried woman careth for the things of the Lord, that she may be holy both in body and in spirit: but she that is married careth for the things of the world, how she may please her husband. And this I speak for your own profit; not that I may cast a snare upon you, but for that which is comely, and that ye may attend upon the Lord without distraction."

As humans with the cognitive makeup of God, what we need isn't the *least concerned* attitude associated with the ravens per se but a worldly interest devoid of anxiety and perplexity. God must be worshipped in an atmosphere devoid of disquieting care and distraction. Anything apart from that is sin. As a general antidote to preserve your mind from the care and snare of the world, Paul has this to say.

"Finally, brethren, whatsoever things are true, whatsoever things are honest, whatsoever things are just, whatsoever things are pure, whatsoever things are lovely, whatsoever things are of good report; if there be any virtue, and if there be any praise, think on these things." (Phil. 4:8)

God's promises should keep you from worry. You must be content with the things that you have. The past is behind and can't be recalled. Tomorrow represents your future, and it's in God's hand. Any attempt to serve tomorrow will breed anxiety, and that in itself is sin. Be content with what you have and give no place for covetousness in your daily vocabulary. A bloated desire for wealth takes you into the debilitating realm of envy. If you envy those who have more than you, that's sin. The sin of covetousness must not be permitted to find a fortress in your conversation.

"Let your conversation be without covetousness; and be content with such things as ye have: for he hath said, I will never leave thee, nor forsake thee" (Heb.13:5).

Divine providence should keep you from worry. Since creation, God's providential goodness has been the preserve for His chosen. In His infinite mercy and providence, God generously provided for you those basic needs of life, namely food, shelter, and clothing. If, for any reason, you failed to trust Him for continuing sustainability, the burden of guilt is solely on you and has nothing to do with Jehovah-Jireh, the great provider.

Consider the fowls

"Behold the fowls of the air: for they sow not, neither do they reap, nor gather into barns; yet your heavenly Father feedeth them. Are ye not much better than they? (Matt. 6:26)

And why take ye thought for raiment? Consider the lilies of the field, how they grow; they toil not, neither do they spin: (Matt. 6:28)

Wherefore, if God so clothe the grass of the field, which to day is, and to morrow is cast into the oven, shall he not much more clothe you, O ye of little faith?" (Matt. 6:30)

Irrespective of the weather conditions, God says that you should look at the fowls even the ravens. They are fed with convenient food and food convenient for them in winter and summer. Consider in this instance means that you should go and learn from them. "Go to the ant, thou sluggard; consider her ways, and be wise" (Prov. 6:6). You should learn from that which you see and be wise. Consider that man often prey on the fowl of the air and hardly feed them, yet they are fed even in the harshest of climes. "Then I saw, and considered it well: I looked upon it, and received instruction" (Prov. 24:32).

God's providence extends even to the meanest creatures. If that is the case, how much more will your Heavenly Father bestow the riches of His divine providence upon His elect such as you? God values you more than the fowl, yet He continues to feed them, and so the sparrows refused to shut their mouth. They have continued to sing among the branches, in and out of season. "By them shall the fowls of the heaven have their habitation, which sing among the branches" (Ps. 104:12).

Consider the ravens and be wise. The common denominator among the fowls is that they sing. The sparrow, the ravens, the parrot, the canary, and the pigeons—they all open their mouths wide and sing. They refused to maintain a close mouth. They sing to glorify God. Some of them like the ravens that could mimic you, after hearing you sing in churches, convey the same to the outer heavens. Consider them and be wise.

"For I will give you a mouth and wisdom, which all your adversaries shall not be able to gainsay nor resist" (Luke 21:15). God, who inhabits the praise of His people, provides for them generously. Therefore, open your mouth wide and praise the Lord who provides for you.

Consider the lilies. The lilies don't turn or spin, but they radiate the glory of God every time you look at them. They spread a fragrance of love and peace. God says that you should consider them and be wise. The lilies are frail and inhabit the field. Most importantly, they are grass. If you consider your body or flesh as grasses, then you will understand why God says that you should not spare a thought for tomorrow. The grass today is tomorrow cast into the oven. So is the human flesh. The grave is the human oven. "For all flesh is as grass, and all the glory of man as the flower of grass. The grass withereth, and the flower thereof falleth away" (1 Pet. 1:24).

The lilies are free from all sorts of worries. You toil to earn your clothes, but lilies don't. Understand that God hasn't called you to be idle, for idleness isn't of God. "By much slothfulness the building decayeth; and through idleness of the hands the house droppeth through" (Eccl. 10:18). God encourages diligence in all that we do. Beauty and cosmetics are the least of God's concerns for men. What stands out in God's reckoning for you is knowledge and grace, not beauty.

When Jesus sent the apostles, they returned full of joy and lacked nothing. "And he said unto them, When I sent you without purse, and scrip, and shoes, lacked ye anything? And they said, Nothing" (Luke 22:35).

Worry should be cast on God

The Bee Gees was a successful musical group formed in 1958. They recorded so many hit songs, among which was one of my all-time favorites, "Rest Your Love on Me," released in 1979. Listen to these few anchor lines on the lyrics.

"Lay your troubles on my shoulder
Put your worries in my pocket
Rest your love on me awhile."

Whenever I listen to those lines, I hear the still small voice of the Lord via the instrumentalists of the Bee Gees. You are at liberty to remind me that the song was not sanctified since it was not performed by a gospel group. God is the sanctifier. If God chose to speak to the heart of anyone through the voice of such a talented group, then the song remains sanctified. Ditto the singers and, of course, you the listener. God uses simple things to confound the wise. That's His divine prerogative. In those lines of the song resonates the Word of the Lord in my heart. "Commit thy way unto the Lord; trust also in him; and he shall bring it to pass" (Ps. 37:5).

Jesus wants you to lay your troubles on His shoulders. Even your entire burden should be cast upon Him. Psalm 55:22 puts it this way. "Cast thy burden upon the Lord, and he shall sustain thee: he shall never suffer the righteous to be moved." The writer of the Bee Gee song must have been to Sunday school. Elton John wrote "Dear God," and Lionel Richie, "Jesus Is Lord." Both songs remain on my evergreen playlist. No soul can produce such work if not sanctified.

God says when you cast your burden on Him, He will sustain you. It's absolutely certain that God will sustain you. Have no doubt about that, for He will never let you slide, let alone fall. Glory be to God. "Casting all your care upon him; for he careth for you" (1 Pet.5:7).

Personal worries, family worries, worries of the present, worries of tomorrow, worries for others, worries for the church, and much more—all your care is suggestive that the disquieting cares of the believer are many and in assortments of continuing mutations. These sorts of worries are very burdensome and excruciating. Their design is to exert a generous measure for sinful strains in your mind. In that manner, they render your mind unfit for the duty of a delightful service to God. The scripture says, "Serve the Lord with gladness: come before his presence with singing" (Ps. 100:2).

Trust in God is freedom from worry. Trust in the Lord is a duty required of you. Trust Him as you commit yourself to Him in everything.

"Shadrach, Meshach, and Abed-nego, answered and said to the king, O Nebuchadnezzar, we are not careful to answer thee in this matter. If it be so, our God whom we serve is able to deliver us from the burning fiery furnace, and he will deliver us out of thine hand, O king. But if not, be it known unto thee, O king, that we will not serve thy gods, nor worship the golden image which thou hast set up. (Dan. 3:16–18)

The three Hebrew boys reposed themselves in God and to His love in the most unquiet of time, and He didn't disappoint them.

"Blessed is the man that trusteth in the Lord, and whose hope the Lord is. For he shall be as a tree planted by the waters, and that spreadeth out her roots by the river, and shall not see when heat cometh, but her leaf shall be green; and shall not be careful in the year of drought, neither shall cease from yielding fruit. (Jer. 17:7–8)

Trust in the Lord. He is the enthronement of freedom and abundance in your life.

Intimacy

"If thou seekest her as silver, and searchest her as for hid treasure" (Prov. 2:4).

Communication don't occur when the message is received but when there's a shared meaning. The hunger for shared meaning is the express desire for intimacy and by extension, spiritual bonding. Understanding takes place when there's a shared meaning in the form of spiritual insight or revelation. There must be some sort of spiritual connection and agreement.

Surely there is a part in man that bears witness to the Spirit of God. "The Spirit itself beareth witness with our spirit, that we are the children of God" (Rom. 8:16). As soon as that divine agreement takes place, the logical and undeniable outcome is understanding.

Attainment of intimacy is a process. The process takes the form of question and answer, building of trust and bonding. Traversing through that process makes it possible for those involved to shatter confidences, clear uncertainties, melt, coalesces and bond. It all begins with communication. God in His infinite wisdom poured out Himself and in His words to man.

Sequel to that, God directed you to attend to His word. God is aware that in the course of that relationship, you

GRACE IN HIS BOSOM

would have to respond to the message that you received from Him hence He set forth to give you the conditions for reaching out to Him uninterrupted. God is not a man that He should lie neither the son of man that He should repent (Num. 23:19). He remains the same yesterday, today and forever (Heb. 13:8). God is not subject to changes, for His word is yes and amen. "For all the promises of God in him are yea, and in him Amen, unto the glory of God by us" (2 Cor. 1:20).

The words that God have spoken are not passive but active. They are taskmasters and they are life. God did all of this in order that you may realize that you can't approach Him on your own terms and conditions. It must be according to His will. If your response does not honor God, it will be nothing but noise in the communication channel.

Due to a heart that is desperately wicked and subject to variations; Christ didn't trust man. "But Jesus did not commit himself unto them, because he knew all men" (John 2:24). God is immensely aware of our unreliable nature.

Elements of intimacy

"If you will search for me with all your heart, then you will find me" (Deut. 4:29). Psychologists agree that love has three important components: passion, intimacy, and commitment. Passion is an intense desire for another person or something. Intimacy is the sharing of feelings, thoughts, needs, desires, and actions with another. Commitment is the willingness to stay with another through thick and thin. "If thou seekest her as silver and searchest for her as for hid treasure" is indeed, the encapsulation in one sentence, of the three distinctive components of love.

In His teachings, Jesus spoke variously regarding those elements. The abide in me and I in you of John 15:4, addressed the issue of passion. "Abide in me, and I in you. As the branch cannot bear fruit of itself, except it abide in the vine; no more can ye, except ye abide in me." On intimacy Jesus said, "I no longer call you servants but friends because I have shared with you all that the father has made known to me" (John 15:15). In respect of commitment, He said, "Greater love than this no one has than to lay down his life for his friend" (John 15:13). In a nutshell, intimacy refers to the deep yearning within you. It is the ability to share mutually and deeply of ourselves with another.

Intimacy with self

The walk of intimacy begins with self. As a matter of necessity, you must develop a deep awareness of yourself. That implies that you must be in touch with your thoughts, attitudes, opinions, emotions, desires, needs, and feelings. It is an attempt to find meaning and integration in your life. A good chunk of intimacy with self has to do with being reflective about your thoughts and feelings at certain moments in the day. That is very important if you must hear from God.

The still small voice often comes as a flow of spontaneous thoughts. If you are not in tune with yourself, you are bound to miss that divine awakening of a voice. Intimacy with yourself is an exercise aimed at sharpening your spiritual antennae to ensure that you pick spiritual signals with relative ease. That's one manner of processing your daily experience.

Dominion is about authority. It is about standing on your covenant heritage to appropriate rulership. Rulership begins with self and the rulership of self begin with your past. You must be able to rule your past. To arrive at self-intimacy, you must be able to conquer your past, for that constitutes the first principle of dominion. Whatever sensor that holds you to your past must be pulled out, not by anyone but you.

Sordid experiences of the past never leave us in a jiffy. The devil knows who you are. If you have not conquered your past by putting it under subjection; Lucifer, the unemployed cherub, will use your past to torment you. The battle of life is not against satan per se. The battle of life is intrinsically against self.

Generally, the quest for intimacy of any sort is the quest for meaning. Without shared meaning, understanding will remain in the domain of hypothesis. It is important to be reflective of your daily experiences. In practical terms, you must ask yourself such questions as, what happened to me at the office today? Why did it happen? How did I react? Who said what and to whom? What was the effect?

You must understand that circumstances and issues have no control over you. The only thing that controls you is your reaction. In life, conflict is inevitable whereas combat is an option. That option must be exercised according to the will of God. God's will is found in His word.

The scripture in Ephesians 4:26–27 says, "Be ye angry, and sin not: let not the sun go down upon your wrath: Neither give place to the devil." Also, "Be not hasty in thy spirit to be angry: for anger resteth in the bosom of fools" (Eccles. 7:9). Again, "An angry man stirreth up strife, and a furious man aboundeth in transgression" (Prov. 29:22).

As you become reflective and begin to process your daily experiences, you will discover that answers will begin to pop up. At the very defining moment when you ask; what is the meaning of all these things? You are just a step away from understanding. "And all they that heard it wondered at those things which were told them by the shepherds. But Mary kept all these things, and pondered them in her heart" (Luke 2:18–19). Others wondered at those things which they heard but Mary kept all these things and pondered them in her heart. The rest heard and wondered.

The things of God are usually a wonder to unbelievers. To you that are within they are signs. Mary kept them in her heart and processed them and pondered the meaning of "all these things." I reckon that all these things still exist today, wherever you find yourself. To others around, it may be a wonder of little or no consequence. However, for you, it is a sign that must be kept in the heart and pondered over.

Personal insight. Personal insight is an understanding of what we think and how we feel, why we reacted the way we did. With personal insight comes the noticeable expression of the Holy Spirit within you. Understand that God will not work with you if you are unwilling to work with Him. As soon as you become reflective with a sharp, spiritual antennae and an obedient heart, God will begin to shed more light upon your life.

In the context of that, understanding is wrought and meaning provided to past experiences. With meaning comes understanding. Nonetheless, it is imperative that you roll together all the life experiences which have become a controlling factor in you. Controlling factors are strongholds. When that happens, a change has occurred which in turn usher in intimacy with self.

Haven achieved the desired awareness and closeness with yourself, that part of you (spirit) that bears witness to the Spirit of God (Holy Spirit), which dwell in you had been sensitized and put on red alert to play its ordained role. That settled, you are well positioned to focus on the feelings and flow of thoughts taking place within you as you interact with others.

Self as major distraction. Intimacy with self is very important. Until we crucify self, we may be far from acceptable worship. Self is a major distraction in worship. You must deal with the anxieties, the worries, the opinions, and comments, to arrive at the threshold of acceptable worship with God. Intimacy with self helps you to define boundaries and set limits. It is a journey in self search and discovery which in turn produces a dominant character postulation. The seeking and searching which God appeals to us to do must begin with self. When you arrive at that point, you become a worthy and sanctified vessel for His usage.

Change within self. There are three stages to arrive at intimacy with self: (1) shattering of confidence, (2) clearing of self-uncertainty, (3) forging ahead as one indivisible self. Going through the aforementioned changes define change. At stage one, the refrigerator of your past experiences is unplugged and left to melt. Stage two is to allow the melted liquid items to mix and coalesce. Every self-imposed stronghold must be permitted to melt. It is an act of the will embedded in your decision. Lastly, the refrigerator is switched back on and the items solidify as one. In all, it is a worthy journey into introspection that shatters pride, punctures ego, evicts unforgiveness and produces humility.

Pride is a virus and God detests it. God detests the pride. He gives grace to the simple. God desires that we purge ourselves of pride, deflate every inflated ego as we get into the level of intimacy with Him.

Two things that happen when you achieve intimacy with self included: (1) a subjective highlight of inner consciousness with God, (2) inner sensitivity to sin. The consciousness constantly presents the picture of two warring kingdoms. That in itself assist you to match forward like a soldier of Christ toward a glorious Christian life and living—for darkness must give way to light. With everything which constitutes a barrier to fellowship with God out of the way, you become set for intimacy with God.

Dealing with trust deficits

Man is fraught with trust deficits and God has to get it out of the way. Little wonder why the journey of intimacy is fraught with trials, and tribulations, successes, and temptations. Notwithstanding, it is a journey worth undertaking.

GRACE IN HIS BOSOM

There's no trespassing God and no shortcuts or circumvention either. Jesus "must need go through Samaria" and He did as scripture says. Therefore, you must go through your own Samaria. After all, Jesus says you must carry your cross and follow Him.

God described understanding as silver and hid treasure. Silver doesn't come easy and hid treasure demands precious sacrifice of time, effort and high risk. Treasures are highly prized and wherever they are kept is often fortified.

Living in that place called grace is free but you must need get there. Understanding is a resident of the city called grace. Grace is that wealthy place which God promised to bring you to. However, you can't get there without passing through fire and water. "For thou, O God, hast proved us: thou hast tried us, as silver is tried. Thou broughtest us into the net; thou laidst affliction upon our loins. Thou hast caused men to ride over our heads; we went through fire and through water: but thou broughtest us out into a wealthy place" (Ps. 66:10–12).

As God takes you through His fire and water experience, certain things such as time, resources and investments will either collapse or perish. At the end, it is what stood the test of God that confronts the treasures. That's God's way of dealing with the trust deficit inherent in man.

Again, consider the experience of the man Job. God allowed Job to go through fire and water. Many things of Job and in Job perished. At the end, God collapsed time and banished efforts to bring Job to the wealthy place.

A comparison of Job chapters 1 and 42 shows that Job got back in double portion, everything that he lost. "And the LORD turned the captivity of Job, when he prayed for his friends: also the LORD gave Job twice as much as he had before" (Job 42:10).

In all, Job became a stronger and more resolute man in fellowship with God. As the water washes and the fire burns up the stronghold and debris of your life, pride gives way to humility and patience.

> Therefore being justified by faith, we have peace with God through our Lord Jesus Christ: By whom also we have access by faith into this grace wherein we stand, and rejoice in hope of the glory of God. And not only so, but we glory in tribulations also: knowing that tribulation worketh patience; And patience, experience; and experience, hope: And hope maketh not ashamed; because the love of God is shed abroad in our hearts by the Holy Ghost which is given unto us. works patience. (Rom. 5:1–5)

Job had overflowing faith in his Redeemer but lacked knowledge. God acknowledged his faith for it is in the eternal honor of God to acknowledge faith even when it is ill-motivated.

Tribulation works patience and patience is a virtue in God's kingdom. The end of a matter is better than the beginning. "Better is the end of a thing than the beginning thereof: and the patient in spirit is better than the proud in spirit" (Eccles. 7:8).

Complete surrender

It is imperative that you arrive at the point of absolute surrender to God. The point where every form of communication with God will revolve around that wonderful serenity prayer: "Lord grant me the serenity to accept the things I cannot change, the courage to change the things I can and the wisdom to know the difference." After that, you can be sure to flow in inner peace and contentment with yourself.

The walk of intimacy is not only expected to deal with warm feelings but also the difficult feelings, disagreements, and differences. It is not possible that you should simply consign the past to the past. You must pass through it as Jesus passed through Samaria to break many barriers and strongholds that brought about the great revival (John 4:4–42).

"And many of the Samaritans of that city believed on him for the saying of the woman, which testified, He told me all that ever I did" (John 4:39). Notice the pattern of the conversation between Jesus and the woman. It was more of a question-and-answer session, which invariably fulfills the three major components of arrival to intimacy.

First, the conversation started with something of a common interest—water. Second, confidences were shattered when Jesus revealed her ugly past to her. Uncertainties were cleared when Jesus expounded to her that worship is not about location or geographical profile but pointedly about "the Father in spirit and in truth." But the hour cometh, and now is, when the true worshippers shall worship the Father in spirit and in truth: for the Father seeketh such to worship him" (John 4:23).

God is a Spirit and they that worship Him must do so in Spirit and in truth. Following that revelation, brokenness manifested in the woman, oneness of Spirit forged ahead and the great revival broke forth.

How sweet it is to follow Jesus who will lead you through every Samaria of your life. It is not possible to circumvent your Samaria and expect to break down the barriers that have held the fulfillment of your glorious destiny in Christ.

Whenever the yearning for meaning in your life is fulfilled, you are in a hurry just like the Samaritan woman; to spread The Good News. Without intimacy with God, discipleship will be hindered. It is the stuck of disciples to share the Word of God with a sense of urgency propelled by joy and fulfillment.

Intimacy with God

Intimacy with God develops over time. Talking regularly to God about your successes, failures, frustrations, and desires is central to the evolvement of spiritual intimacy. As matter of priority, a building of trust is critical and that omes through honest disclosures to God.

Conversation is the bedrock of meaning. Put differently, meaning comes out of conversation. Without meaning, there can never be understanding.

In Isaiah 1:18, God says, "Come now, and let us reason together, saith the LORD: though your sins be as scarlet, they shall be as white as snow; though they be red like crimson, they shall be as wool." Reasoning connotes conversation on the highest frequency. It's intensive conversation. That's what God desires from you.

The invitation of Isaiah 1:18 is similar to that of Jeremiah 33:3, which says, "Call unto me, and I will answer thee, and show thee great and mighty things which thou knowest not." The Bible is full of such invitations from a loving Father to his sons and daughters for the purpose of bringing you closer to Him.

God expects that you should talk regularly to Him, about yourself and/or any information about Him that you need clarification. Your open and honest quest for the meaning of past experiences and present occurrences usher in insightful revelations.

The Holy Spirit who knows the things of God even the deep things of the Lord will begin to share the meaning of such occurrences or messages with that part of you that bears witness with the Spirit of God.

Understanding is the logical product of a shared meaning: the breaking forth of light, revealing. "For the LORD giveth wisdom: out of his mouth cometh knowledge and understanding" (Prov. 2:6). God is in wait for your earnest quest for meaning. The invitations are lying in wait. You have to make the move by opening your mouth to ask.

Your sincere and honest quest for meaning of unresolved and unspoken experiences prompted God to speak, responding with knowledge and understanding.

Nonetheless, intimacy cannot be sustained without commitment. Also, it is not possible to reap the fruits of intimacy without responsibility. You can have a wedding without commitment but you can't have a marriage without responsibility.

Without responsibility, the benefits of marriage are lost. Commitment breeds responsibility which in turn, delivers dividend. The fruits of intimacy include anointing, dominion, understanding, joy, and answered prayers.

Your place before God

God is continually looking out for a good man. Some speak and we are helped. Others say the same thing and we are empty. The difference lies in the men themselves. Spiritual things are never carried in the head. We lay in wait upon good words but God seeks good men. Nothing can be a substitute for what a man is before God. The man is central to God's divine agenda. For many people, trouble comes first, followed by desperation, experience, and life. Thereafter, comes doctrine. "Blessed is the man that endureth temptation: for when he is tried, he shall receive the crown of life, which the Lord hath promised to them that love him" (James 1:12).

GRACE IN HIS BOSOM

Specific Ministry

Specific ministries do not come first by doctrine but by life experience. Abraham learned faith by experience and not by doctrine. Our special experience of Christ is what constitutes our ministry. The trial of our faith works in experience. "It is a faithful saying: For if we be dead with him, we shall also live with him" (2 Tim. 2:11).

Do not envy the man with a specific ministry. To receive a specific ministry is costly and the price enormous. Only those who pay the price receive the costly ministry, for life is released through death and only so. For to live is to die. "Confirming the souls of the disciples, and exhorting them to continue in the faith, and that we must through much tribulation enter into the kingdom of God" (Acts 14:22).

Also consider this, "For ye are dead, and your life is hid with Christ in God" (Col. 3:3). A life that is hid with Christ in God is indeed a triumphant life.

Consequently, your specific ministry which is borne out of intimate relationship with God constitutes the knowledge of Christ acquired through the way He has led you. What you minister is life that the Spirit formed in you, hence it is appropriate to say that God doesn't use the inexperience.

Abide in me.

Addressing His disciples, says, "I am the true vine, and my Father is the husband-man. Every branch in me that beareth not fruit he taketh away: and every branch

> that beareth fruit, he purgeth it, that it may bring forth more fruit. Now ye are clean through the word which I have spoken unto you. I am the vine, ye are the branches: He that abideth in me, and I in him, the same bringeth forth much fruit: for without me ye can do nothing. (John 15:1–5)

Affliction and trial is synonymous with the purging of the branch. There are rich blessings that are inherent in every trial and affliction. Such is the design of the Father for increased awareness and spiritual sensitivity. The sole purpose is to make us acceptable vessels for communion with Him.

In affliction, the work of the Holy Spirit is immensely magnified. By drawing us into close union with God the Son and God the Father, the Comforter bring us into the threshold of comfort. God loves us and the heart of the Father is revealed in the Son. As you abide in Christ, you rest in the comfort of the grace in The Father's bosom.

Blessing in obedience

God cherishes relationships. He gave His only begotten Son that man may have life and have it more abundantly. The blessing of the Lord is upon the man who is in an intimate relationship with God and that blessing rides on the crest of obedience. Granted, you got faith. Your faith impels you to believe. Believe propels you to obey.

Obedience attracts blessing and blessing expels poverty. The blessing of the Lord maketh rich and adds no sorrow. The gifts and callings of God are without repentance. Once given, God doesn't regret it. Every blessing is in obedience.

Obedience connotes a response. It implies action. Obedience is active and not dormant. When a son obeys the father, he brings joy to the father. A happy father is one that is eager to bless the son.

God our Father says, "My son attend to my word" (Prov. 2:1). God's word is His instruction to you His son. Your obedience as God's chosen son must be visible in your response to His word. Your blessing is only a response away from your obedience. Therefore, obey God and leave all the consequences to Him.

Boosters of Intimacy

The work of intimacy is never complete without the following boosters which enable you to deal with the trust deficits and come to the state of absolute certainty with God and His promises. They are (1) the Word, (2) Holy Spirit, (3) worship, (4) prayer.

The Word

God poured out Himself in His own words as recorded in the Bible. He expects that you should know Him first via His word. His word is alive. His word is life. Also, God intends that you approach Him on the basis of

His word. The Word of God is spoken to cause changes. Transformations such as that is, wrapped in intimacy.

God bestowed eternal honor on His word. "I will worship toward thy holy temple, and praise thy name for thy lovingkindness and for thy truth: for thou hast magnified thy word above all thy name" (Ps. 138:2). God honors His word above all the names that you call Him.

By reading the Bible, we learn about the character of God, His ability, and His will. His love for you do not change simply because you read the Bible. He first loved you before time. When you receive His word, you learn to love Him. "We love him, because he first loved us" (1 John 4:19). That way, intimacy is stimulated and deepened.

In Proverbs 2:1, God expressly requested you to receive His word and hide it in your heart. It is important that you store, save, and preserve and protect the Word of God in your heart. That is important because the primary vocation of Satan is to twist the Word of God.

Little wonder Jesus called Satan the father of lies. "Ye are of your father the devil, and the lusts of your father ye will do. He was a murderer from the beginning, and abode not in the truth, because there is no truth in him. When he speaketh a lie, he speaketh of his own: for he is a liar, and the father of it" (John 8:44).

The Word of God in your heart is like a beacon of crystal bright stone raised against the barrage of demonic contraptions that constantly invades your thought process every moment.

David hid the word in his heart that he might not sin against God. "Thy word have I hid in mine heart, that I might not sin against thee" (Ps. 119:11). You can't develop intimacy with God without getting acquainted with His written word. Your knowledge of the written word prepares you for a bedroom setting sort of conversation with The Messiah.

Conversation is the seed for understanding. It's important that you read the Bible first because in the course of your conversation, God will be referring you to His word. Against that backdrop, He invited you to come let us reason together (Isa. 1:18).

Reasoning is a constructive and thoughtful process. God is not pleased with thoughtless and careless words or statements. Perfunctory and vain babbling constitutes distractions. Reasoning is a penetrating art that involves the six senses hence the whole body and soul is engaged. God wants you to keep your body and soul a living sacrifice acceptable unto Him. God, reasons with you on the standpoint of your anger, frustrations, grief, fear, confusion, and contradictions. Sanctify yourself with the Word of God. That way, your worship will be meaningful.

The Holy Spirit

Jesus began His public preaching this manner. "The Spirit of the Lord is upon me, because he hath anointed me to preach the gospel to the poor; he hath sent me to heal the brokenhearted, to preach deliverance to the captives, and recovering of sight to the blind, to set at liberty them that are bruised" (Luke 4:18). The Holy Spirit is a gift from God. The promise of the Holy Spirit is to everyone who believes. The Holy Spirit is your guide, your comforter and counselor. The Holy Spirit is to enable you have divine illumination by bringing the Word of God to life.

The experience of the Holy Spirit is deep and personal. There cannot be a better description of the role and benefits associated with the Holy Spirit than that provided in Isaiah 11:2. "And the spirit of the LORD shall rest upon him, the spirit of wisdom and understanding, the spirit of counsel and might, the spirit of knowledge and of the fear of the LORD."

The seven dimensions of the Holy Spirit depicted in that scripture points toward one thing: intimacy. None of those range or dimension of Spirit can come upon anyone without an intimate relationship with the Lord. It is not possible to profit from the joy of intimacy without the Holy Spirit.

The Holy Spirit is in you and manifests the works of God through you. "Ye are of God, little children, and have overcome them: because greater is he that is in you, than he that is in the world" (1 John 4:4).

The Holy Spirit is the accord concordance. Philippians 2:2 says, "Fulfil ye my joy, that ye be likeminded, having the same love, being of one accord, of one mind." The Holy Spirit crystallizes the bundle of shared experiences in Christ leading to understanding.

Consider the seven dimensions of the Holy Spirit as highlighted in Isaiah 11:2, and you will understand the central role that the Holy Spirit plays in your quest for intimacy and spiritual understanding. (1) The Spirit of the Lord, (2) the Spirit of wisdom, (3) the Spirit of understanding, (4) the Spirit of counsel, (5) the Spirit of power, (6) the Spirit of knowledge, (7) the Spirit of the fear of the Lord.

These seven dimensions of the Holy Spirit rolled together and invested in you is *grace*. The walk of intimacy and the logical conclusion of the Christian journey is destination Grace. Grace is the governing influence of God, encapsulated and invested in you as favor.

Again, the Holy Spirit can cause you to discern something concerning another person, making it possible for a prophetic declaration to spring from your heart. Prophetic words draw people closer to God. Prophesy is God speaking directly to you. Whenever prophecy confronts what you are going through, you have no option than to fall at the feet of Jesus and worship.

Worship

Worship is central in God's agenda for you. Worship is intricately linked with obedience and knowledge. It is dangerous to worship someone or something that you do not know. That is why God wants you to know Him before you worship. The reverse is never His intention for you.

Everything you desire from God is obtained on the platform of worship. In Exodus 23:25 the scripture says, "And ye shall serve the LORD your God, and he shall bless thy bread, and thy water; and I will take sickness away from the midst of thee." Joshua recognized the importance of worship and declared, "As for me and my household, we shall serve the LORD." Job 36:11 puts it this way, "If they obey and serve him, they shall spend their days in prosperity, and their years in pleasure."

Your service to God is an act of obedience. You worship God with your talents, time, and treasure. Your act of obedience is most noticeable in worship which is not synonymous with singing and dancing. Worship involves setting aside quality time for God.

Worship takes you into the threshold of intimacy. Worship is the largest marketplace for anointing and it is obtained cheaply. Praise and thanksgiving are part of worship. The Lord dwells in the praises of His people. "But thou art holy, O thou that inhabitest the praises of Israel" (Ps. 22:3). Worship builds intimacy with God.

Prayer

Prayer is a form of communication. It is a way of reaching out to God in heavenly places. God is Spirit and they that worship Him must do so in Spirit and in truth (John 4:24). Prayer is your response to God who spoke variously before time on every aspect of your life on earth. God knew that you would at some points in time respond, hence He left an open door through the channel of prayers, so that you can reach Him.

You pray because you have spiritual needs which are beyond your capacity and ability as a human. Consciousness of your spiritual needs springs from reading the Bible. In Matthew 5:3; Jesus commended those who are conscious of their spiritual need. "Blessed are the poor in spirit: for theirs is the kingdom of heaven." The Bible is replete with

GRACE IN HIS BOSOM

many faithfuls who prayed. Prayer suggests a relationship postulation. You pray because you trust the one you are praying to. You pray because you yearn for guidance, wisdom, and understanding. Above all, you pray because you need answers to questions that seem beyond your limited human comprehension.

Generally, prayer draws you closer to God and fosters intimacy. Daniel prayed to the Lord his God and confessed the sins of his people (Dan. 9:4). One vital key to successful prayer is that you must know to whom your prayer is directed to. Second, you must know His will. Also, you must come to prayer with your strong points.

Lastly, you must present your request according to His will. Prayers offered according to God's will, exercised in faith and sealed in the name of Jesus, have over the ages proven effective. Prayer draws you closer to God and deepens intimacy.

Purpose

Every manufacturer determines the purpose for which a product is made prior to it being released to the market. The consumer will buy that product if it satisfies his needs. God is not a manufacturer. He is the Creator. He created man even as He determined the purpose.

According to 2 Timothy 1:9, "Who hath saved us, and called us with an holy calling, not according to our works, but according to his own purpose and grace, which was given us in Christ Jesus before the world began." God saved you expressly for His purpose. It is not about you. It is about Him and His Kingdom.

Consequently, "And we know that all things work together for good to them that love God, to them who are the called according to his purpose" (Rom. 8:28). The discovery of purpose constitutes the greatest challenge of mankind. It is very important. Purpose is encased in your vision. When God gives you a vision, His purpose for your life is located in that vision. Until you step out into that vision, you can't live out the purpose of God for you.

Purpose is active. Purpose is practical. Purpose is doing. Purpose is obtained at the thrashing field. Lingering and procrastination strangles purpose. Lot was one man that lingered. He lingered the very morning that Sodom was to be destroyed but grace found him. The account in Genesis 19:16 says, "And while he lingered, the men laid hold upon his hand, and upon the hand of his wife, and upon the hand of his two daughters; the LORD being merciful unto him: and they brought him forth, and set him without the city." The Angels rescued Lot and propelled him toward the mountain that is destined to be his thrashing field but Lot decided for proximity and convenience.

Convenience will minimize your purpose. God honored Lot's plea to settle for a "little one" in the low lying plain instead of the big picture which the mountains represent. Unlike Uncle Abraham, Lot was scared of the unknown and couldn't move against his fears to fulfill purpose.

The purpose for your life is that your life should count for something for God. It is at the thrashing field that God begins to drop a handful of your purpose. The vision is for an appointed time. Waiting is an important aspect of realizing your vision. At the appointed time, the Spirit of the Lord will nudge you into the thrashing field where you begin to live out His purpose for your life. Time is now to step into your destiny. It's about every day doing what God has called you to do. You must live out God's calling, His gift, His destiny for your life.

Brokenness. The clay vessel broke; it "was marred." Put differently, the vessel was impaired, disfigured or spoiled both in appearance and quality. But God didn't pick up another material to make a new one. The Potter used the same clay, same material that was broken to make it yet another.

Brokenness is a condition for the containment of the treasures of God. If you must be an instrument of change in the hand of God, you must undergo, willingly, death. All the false self, the pride, the vulgar-induced vanity and security must give way. Your heart, soul, and mind must come to agreement that you have given up everything that you cling to, as they relate to false comfort and safety.

The weaker the vessel, the stronger the power. That's the mystery. Brokenness in humility is the consecration that you need for the enactment of the vision of God in you. To model Christ to the world, demand that you abandon all safety and security except those rooted in God.

Bonding

The logical destination of the kingdom journey is love. Listen to Jesus.

> If ye abide in me, and my words abide in you, ye shall ask what ye will, and it shall be done unto you. Herein is my Father glorified, that ye bear much fruit; so shall ye be my disciples. As the Father hath loved me, so have I loved you: continue ye in my love. If ye keep my commandments, ye shall abide in my love; even as I have kept my Father's commandments, and abide in his love. (John 15:7–10)

Jesus charges you to live, continue and remain in His love. If you are saved, you are in Christ. "There is therefore now no condemnation to them which are in Christ Jesus, who walk not after the flesh, but after the Spirit" (Rom. 8:1). Abiding in Christ is your position as a true believer.

The shared experience in Christ guarantees that you are held securely in a permanent relationship. The common field of experience confirms that you hear His voice and obey His commandments.

GRACE IN HIS BOSOM

Obedience to the commandments of Christ is proof that you have arrived at destination Grace. "And he that keepeth his commandments dwelleth in him, and he in him. And hereby we know that he abideth in us, by the Spirit which he hath given us" (1 John 3:24).

God abides in us, by the Spirit which He has given us. The Scripture in Amos 3:3 is an important question. "Can two walk together, except they be agreed?"

Oftentimes, we assume that the verse under reference speaks of two people that are physically in contact with each other. That is wrong. God is talking about agreement with Him, because He is Spirit and God. Also, God in His infinite wisdom, called you god. "I have said, Ye are gods; and all of you are children of the most High" (Ps. 82:6).

Consequently, God is saying, when the Spirit of God meets the Spirit of God, dwelling in the inside of you-god; there should be agreement. Notice the word *walk* in Amos 3:3. The same word was used to describe the relationship between God and Noah. "These are the generations of Noah: Noah was a just man and perfect in his generations, and Noah walked with God" (Noah 6:9).

To walk with God instead of work for God entails a Spirit-to-Spirit relationship. At the point of interwoven, intermingling, interlocking, coalescing, and ventilation of the Spirit(s); nothing that you ever asked, would be withheld from you. "The wind bloweth where it listeth, and thou hearest the sound thereof, but canst not tell whence it cometh, and whither it goeth: so is every one that is born of the Spirit" (John 3:8).

In Matthew 18:20, Jesus expanded Amos 3:3 to complete the Trinity. "For where two or three are gathered together in my name, there am I in the midst of them."

Here is the icing on the cake: the name of Jesus. The name above every other name. "Wherefore God also hath highly exalted him, and given him a name which is above every name: That at the name of Jesus every knee should bow, of things in heaven, and things in earth, and things under the earth; And that every tongue should confess that Jesus Christ is Lord, to the glory of God the Father" (Phil. 2:9–11). Jesus says, "My words are Spirit and they are life."

The Bible is like a bag of seeds unto us. The seeds, the promises are for your planting in your spirit man garden. As soon as there is agreement between the divine seeds which is spirit and life with your spirit-man, the seed will spring up and grow. There should be no restrictions, whatsoever. The seed will become a tree and a forest. "It is the spirit that quickeneth; the flesh profiteth nothing: the words that I speak unto you, they are spirit, and they are life" (John 6:63).

"Abide in me, and I in you. As the branch cannot bear fruit of itself, except it abide in the vine; no more can ye, except ye abide in me. I am the vine, ye are the branches: He that abideth in me, and I in him, the same bringeth forth much fruit: for without me ye can do nothing" (John 15:4–5).

Salvation is everything. It is your pivotal union with Christ. Salvation accounts for your productive life as a believer. In the absence of that vital union, you can do nothing. Salvation that comes by grace is also maintained by grace. "O foolish Galatians, who hath bewitched you, that ye should not obey the truth, before whose eyes Jesus Christ hath been evidently set forth, crucified among you? This only would I learn of you, Received ye the Spirit by the works of the law, or by the hearing of faith? Are ye so foolish? having begun in the Spirit, are ye now made perfect by the flesh?" (Gal. 3:1–3).

Bonding does not save. Spiritual bonding is the terminal sign of salvation. When Jesus called you friends, that was intimacy. Oftentimes, people describe their relationship as intimate friends. That is absolutely correct. You cannot be friends without intimacy. Forget the notion about casual friendship. It is either you are friends or not.

Jesus demonstrates that in John 15:15. "Henceforth I call you not servants; for the servant knoweth not what his lord doeth: but I have called you friends; for all things that I have heard of my Father I have made known unto you." Friendship, like marriage, is expected to lead you into secrets of each other.

On the other hand, you can be friendly to each other without bonding. An unborn baby is said to have bonded with the mother for the duration of the pregnancy. During that period, the baby does nothing but is sustained by whatever comes through the mother.

When Jesus began to speak of "Abide in me and I in you." He took the relationship beyond friendship into the realm of spiritual bonding. Before you cry that such is not possible, because there is no way the spirit of a sinful man can bond with a Holy God; let me remind you that God already called you gods and Christ in you. "Ye are of God, little children, and have overcome them: because greater is he that is in you, than he that is in the world" (1 John 4:4). Christ in you the hope of glory. God wants you to be still in His presence just like the unborn child in the mother's womb. Only then will you know that He is God (Ps. 46:10).

Google describes bonding as "the establishment of a relationship or link with someone based on shared feelings, interests, or experiences." That's bonding as a noun. Bonding as an adjective is described as "having the function or effect of establishing a relationship or link with someone based on shared feelings, interests, or experiences." Happily, both bonding as a noun and an adjective apply to faith people like you and me.

In a nutshell, bonding is not just the coming together of a matter or people but there is a third agent, indeed, a link. For us, the Holy Spirit is the "bonding agent." Put succinctly, the Holy Spirit is the divine seal that binds believers to Christ. The same seal bond between believers.

Therefore, it is bonding to pray and to worship together because the Spirit that blows where it chooses and no one knows where it comes from or gets to is at work, and of such is you that is born of the Spirit (John 3:8). In all of that, the Holy Spirit is the facilitator. It comes like a heat cloven tongue of fire or mighty rushing chariot of wind from heaven.

There is no better way to describe the experience of Acts 2 than spiritual bonding.

> And when the day of Pentecost was fully come, they were all with one accord in one place. And suddenly there came a

> sound from heaven as of a rushing mighty wind, and it filled all the house where they were sitting. And there appeared unto them cloven tongues like as of fire, and it sat upon each of them. And they were all filled with the Holy Ghost, and began to speak with other tongues, as the Spirit gave them utterance. (Acts 2:1–4).

It came with fire, heat, pressure, and wind. Those are the elements required to seal anything. Together, they constitute the divine escort. As soon as the sealing was over, the Apostles manifested in diverse dimensions, the god in them. Diverse miracles happened and souls were saved to the glory of God.

Again, the sharing of a common field of experience is a condition for bonding. The experience of salvation, baptism, communion, studying the word, fasting, praying, worship, believe, faith, giving, obedience, love, patience, humility, forgiveness, and all that constitutes our common heritage in Christ.

In Ezekiel 20:37, God made a stunning statement. "And I will cause you to pass under the rod, and I will bring you into the bond of the covenant." Dreadful as the scripture sounds, it is meant to bond you with God.

As the shepherd permits the sheep to pass under his rod and through a narrow gate, so it is with Jesus, the Good Shepherd; who says I know my sheep and they hear my voice. Passing under the rod is one manner of accounting for the flock as well as disciplining the errant sheep. It is the pruning of the vine branch so that it can bring forth more fruit.

The bond of covenant is the work of Grace that binds us to God. We are His people and He is our God. Conviction binds us like a cord to God and we will never desire to escape. On the other hand, God will never leave you nor forsake you. That's a covenant, even the covenant of peace. "For the mountains shall depart, and the hills be removed; but my kindness shall not depart from thee, neither shall the covenant of my peace be removed, saith the LORD that hath mercy on thee" (Isa. 54:10).

When you abide in Christ and Christ in you, you have accessed the rest that remains to the people of God. "There remaineth therefore a rest to the people of God. For he that is entered into his rest, he also hath ceased from his own works, as God did from his. Let us labour therefore to enter into that rest, lest any man fall after the same example of unbelief" (Heb. 4:9–11). You have ceased from your own works. You are now having a walk with God as it was in the garden in the cool of the day (Gen. 3:8).

Grace has entered and you are increasingly aware of divine presence within your life. First John 4:13 puts it adequately, "Hereby know we that we dwell in him, and he in us, because he hath given us of his Spirit." The governing influence of God that makes things to happen on their own accord is now prevalent in your life. Another name for that is grace.

Absence of habitual sin in your life is a proof that you abide in Christ. "Whosoever abideth in him sinneth not: whosoever sinneth hath not seen him, neither known him"

GRACE IN HIS BOSOM

(1 John 3:6). Habitual sin is one that so easily besets you. It was a routine before it graduated to a habit. Until you lay it aside, you are far from spiritual bonding. "Wherefore seeing we also are compassed about with so great a cloud of witnesses, let us lay aside every weight, and the sin which doth so easily beset us, and let us run with patience the race that is set before us" (Heb. 12:1). Besetting sins are such that they so easily entangle us. Habitual sins are like sweet candy. They are a great distraction to the kingdom journey. I leave the examples to your imagination. They are so common to you such that you may no longer consider them as sins.

Following the example of Jesus is the final proof that you abide in Him. "He that saith he abideth in him ought himself also so to walk, even as he walked" (1 John 2:6).

Prior to His ascension into heaven, Jesus left us with a marching order, generally called the Great Commission. He commissioned us to model Him to the world. "Go ye therefore, and teach all nations, baptizing them in the name of the Father, and of the Son, and of the Holy Ghost: Teaching them to observe all things whatsoever I have commanded you: and, lo, I am with you alway, even unto the end of the world. Amen (Matt. 28:19–20). In a nutshell, Jesus asked us to go to the world and model Him. He commissioned us models and living epistles.

But what makes Christ our model?

> Though I speak with the tongues of men
> and of angels, and have not charity, I am
> become as sounding brass, or a tinkling

cymbal. And though I have the gift of prophecy, and understand all mysteries, and all knowledge; and though I have all faith, so that I could remove mountains, and have not charity, I am nothing. And though I bestow all my goods to feed the poor, and though I give my body to be burned, and have not charity, it profiteth me nothing. (1 Cor. 13:1–3)

There are two important kingdom tools that are critical to the assessment of your kingdom journey. The first is the measure of *love*. That is what I call the weight measure. It deals with the depth or volume. The other is the measure of the *altar*. That, I refer to as the linear measure. It is the length and width. The altar that you serve is expected to speak for you.

Throughout his kingdom journey, Abraham built altars. Ditto Isaac and Jacob. Altars are necessary for the assessment of your kingdom commitment. One thing that is common to both volume and the linear measure is the scale. Obedience is the ratio of kingdom commitment. It is the scale measure. When your obedience is directly proportional to your kingdom commitment, the result is a convergence of kingdom fulfillment known as overflow. You become an overcomer indeed. Nonetheless, half obedience is considered as disobedience in the Kingdom. Complete and total obedience is what is required. "And now abideth faith, hope, charity, these three; but the greatest of these is charity" (1 Cor. 13:13). As a believer, it is important that your measure of *love* (your weight, your volume) must fit into your *altar* (your space-length and breadth). Put differently, the X and Y must be occupied or filled by the volume Z. The result is XYZ, which translates to 3D (three-dimension). The 3D is a model. Model is three-dimensional. A picture is two dimensional hence not a model. In mathematical terms any two-dimensional object is described along the XY axis. To become a model you must introduce the Z factor which accounts for the 3D. The Z remains the depth, height, or volume.

Love or charity is like the Z factor. The passage in 1 Corinthians 13:1 above made it explicitly clear that no matter what you do or become, without love you are as empty as a synchronized noisy vessel "as sounding brass, or a tinkling cymbal." You may have diverse gifts and calling but without love, you are nothing. Even giving to the poor and self-sacrifice does not equal love in the divine estimation. Christ is love. He is like the Z factor that fill in the empty yearning of our lives. Love is the terminal destination of the kingdom journey. It is destination grace. God is love. "And above all things have fervent charity among yourselves: for charity shall cover the multitude of sins" (2 Peter 4:8).

Begotten love critical mass

When a limited number of people know something in a new way, it remains the conscious property of only those people. However, there's a point at which if only one more person steps into a new horizon, that new awareness is picked up by everyone. When that occurs, it's a manifestation of the Critical Mass Theory.

God so loved the world that He gave His only BEGOTTEN Son a ransom for mankind. BEGOTTEN is all about sharing God's love. In BEGOTTEN, God's love reached the critical mass. It became eternal-no separation, no end. God's love never perished. Begotten is the sharing of God's love in all and for all and by all who believe. In BEGOTTEN lies the power of love. It is the power to lay it down and to take it up. In BEGOTTEN resonate the power of resurrection. Love is now your new identity. Wear love as a badge of honor. Listen to Jesus: "These things I command you, that ye love one another" (John 15:17). Wear it as a badge of honor. "By this shall all men know that ye are my disciples, if ye have love one to another" (John 13:35).

About the Author

Henry Akweke Fagbola is a director at Covenant Elevation Christian Center (CECC), Bronx, New York. He lives out his passion for teaching the Word of God with a weekly program called Wisdom Hour. He trained at the Word of Faith Bible Institute (WOFBI) in Lagos. He holds an HND in cartography from Kaduna Polytechnic; a PGD in journalism from the Nigerian Institute of Journalism, Lagos; a PGD in management and MBA from the University of Calabar; and a PhD in management and leadership studies from American Bible College University, Avondale, Arizona. He has served as a minister and coordinator for the Satellite Fellowship Program of the Living Faith Church Worldwide (Winners Chapel) Dopemu, Lagos, and a former senior administrator of the Protocol Service Group, Canaanland, Ota (2005). He was the national secretary of the Nigerian Cartographic Association (NCA) (1997–2003) and a resource person to the National Population Commission (NPC) (2006). Dr. Fagbola, a prolific writer, is passionate about sharing the Gospel of Jesus Christ.